HOW TO VOLUNTEER LIKE A PRO

AN AMATEUR'S GUIDE FOR WORKING WITH TEENAGERS

JIM HANCOCK

ZONDERVAN®

youth
specialties

youth
specialties

How to Volunteer Like a Pro: An Amatuer's Guide for Working with Teenagers
Copyright 2009 by Jim Hancock

Youth Specialties resources, 300 S. Pierce St., El Cajon, CA 92020 are published by Zondervan, 5300 Patterson Ave. SE, Grand Rapids, MI 49530.

ISBN 978-0-310-52113-6

Cover design by David Conn
Interior design by Mark Novelli, IMAGO MEDIA

Printed in the United States of America

CONTENTS

INTRODUCTION

After two decades as a professional youth worker, I quit my job in the church and rejoined the ranks of volunteer youth workers—and I loved it!

Walking into a room full of kids I didn't know and doing the honest work of building relationships from scratch—without a business card or position to justify my presence—launched one of the most invigorating and satisfying chapters of my life as a youth worker.

The transition from professional to volunteer gave me reasons to review everything I thought about youth work and everything I did as a youth worker. *Everything.*

I came to understand things as a volunteer I might never have learned as a youth ministry professional. Could I have learned those things without the years I spent as a paid youth worker? I don't know. I'm not sure it matters.

The important thing is sharing the wealth and hoping what I've learned will help you volunteer like a pro.

So...wade in and let me know what you think.

jh
Leucadia, California
j.hancock.web@mac.com

1

AMATEURS

This is an amateur's guide to working with teenagers. Anyone who assumes the word *amateur* means incompetent, unskilled, and inexperienced hasn't been paying attention...

The word *amateur* comes to English via the French, who got it from Italians, who took Latin in high school. The root word is *amator*—that's *lover* in English. Amateurs do what they do because they love it. Amateurs are responsible for Wikipedia, Linux, and Firefox®; amateurs conduct search-and-rescue operations and knock down structural fires in small towns; Olympic-class athletes—most of them—are amateurs.

That's the sense in which I think of volunteer youth workers as amateurs, and in that sense the title "amateur youth worker" is in no way second-class.

If you give up your day off to take kids someplace they think is cool...if you sacrifice weekends or vacation days to be at camp with kids...if you hang out with adolescents *after* you've finished your day job instead of going home to relax or do your laundry, then you're an amateur in youth ministry, and we thank you.

At the end of the day, amateurism may be the only good and sustainable motive for volunteering in youth ministry. (All the other motives seem either bad or unsustainable...more on that later.)

I often hear amateur youth workers say, "Oh, I'm just a volunteer."

Nonsense. The word *just* doesn't belong in the same sentence with the word *volunteer*. Saying "I'm just a volunteer" misses the point entirely. It's like saying, "The Walt Disney Company is a Mickey Mouse operation"—and not in a good way. I became an amateur youth worker *after* I gave up my job as a youth ministry professional. And I guarantee my performance as an amateur met or exceeded what I offered as a professional.

Volunteer youth workers express God's compassion for kids in a way no one else does. Just about every adult who relates to kids does so at least partly because he or she also gets something from the transaction. I'm not saying that's inherently bad. What I'm saying is: if professional schoolteachers, guidance counselors, coaches, music directors, tutors, drama teachers, and youth workers are noble—and they almost always are—then volunteer youth workers who do it for love are saintly. Anyone who says otherwise is not paying attention.

2

THE BEST OF
MOTIVES

There's more than one reason to work with kids and, frankly, some reasons are better than others. In fact, some reasons are no good at all:

- There are adults who gravitate toward younger people because they're uncomfortable with their own peers.

- There are adults who want to be in control and find adolescents easier—if only because so many kids crave attention from adults.

- There are adults who long to atone for the sins of their own youth and want to rescue kids "before it's too late."

- Sad but true, there are adults who are drawn to kids for sexual reasons. (Not all of these are stereotypical pedophiles—some are individuals whose arrested personality development is fixated on adolescent physical ideals and relational patterns.)

- Some adults are *guilted* into volunteering as youth workers.

None of these is on the list of good reasons to engage in student ministries. The Good List looks something like this:

- Adults who want to help kids grow the way *they* were helped back in the day (not in the precise *manner* they were helped but in the fact that an adult was present to help).

- Adults with firsthand knowledge of the challenges kids face—educators, medical and mental health professionals, officers of the court, parents, college students, and young men and women who regard adolescents with empathy and compassion.

- Individuals who pay attention to the dynamics of culture and society with generous insight and appropriate sympathy for adolescent experiences and passages.

- People who sense a call from God (and have their sense of calling ratified by God's people) to serve kids and their families.

It's one thing to pitch in from time to time (and thank God a lot of people do). It's another thing to enter the community of folks we call youth workers—the people whose service in God's kingdom is defined by compassionate engagement in the world of kids.

When someone asks, "Why do you work with adolescents?" or, "Why do you *want* to work with adolescents?" what do you tell them? (And if your answer is somehow less than completely true to your real reasons, why is that?)

3

THE FIRST
DAY

I think the first day as a volunteer is the hardest.

After two decades of professional youth work, the first time I walked into a senior high youth group without a business card, without a title, without a clear idea of what I would be doing there, I felt awkward and excited and on edge. I knew the youth pastor and a couple of other leaders. I didn't know any kids. I surveyed the room. I approached a group of boys who fell silent as I came near. I said hello and tried to strike up a conversation. They gave me their names and schools. Their eyes shifted uncomfortably. "Okay, nice to meet you," I said and moved along to try again.

After several false starts, I retreated to the men's room to regain my composure. I'm an extrovert; this shouldn't be so hard. Returning to the youth room, I was determined not to take refuge in conversation with another adult—that seemed too easy. Mercifully, the youth pastor got the meeting underway; I sat down on the floor with everybody else, the pressure relieved.

What it reminded me of was the first day at a new school—the difference was I *chose* to show up at this meeting. What I was thinking when I agreed to that?

But then I was introduced to the crowd, and I waved and smiled—and afterward a couple of kids made small talk, and that helped me relax. The ice was broken; I made it through the first day.

That was one of several *first days* I've experienced as a volunteer youth worker. Another occurred on a two-and-a-half-hour nighttime bus ride to junior high camp. I knew no one. After trying and failing to get a conversation going with the boy seated next to me, I retreated into the dark and tried to remember all the lyrics to my favorite album when I was that age. I realized I had no favorite album when I was 13. (I mainly listened to AM pop radio and was still trying to decide if I liked the Beatles.) So I worked downstream in my memory until I found a favorite: the obscure but amazing *Vanilla Fudge* album, possibly the greatest collection of cover tunes in history—including two Beatles songs.

That night on the bus I concentrated on getting my mind in the right frame, knowing the silence wouldn't last long once we got to camp because there would be plenty of excuses to talk and plenty to talk about. That's always the way it's been for me. It just takes a little time—measured in minutes, not months—to break through the awkwardness. I think part of the beauty of that sort of cold start is it taught me to feel for the adolescent who walks in alone for the first time. Which in turn makes it easy for me to approach a newcomer and start a conversation so he doesn't have to feel like a stranger one second longer than necessary.

At the end of the day I think friendliness creates the path by which a person moves from outsider to insider in a youth group. And the rules in that context are the same as anywhere else...*almost*.

One difference is there are hardly any adults who get involved with kids outside school hours unless they want something. They are coaches, drama teachers, employers—people who have something to accomplish and need kids to do it. There are also a small number of pedophiles, codependents, and Peter Pan types who seek emotional or sexual gratification from kids. Given that, don't be surprised if kids don't automatically trust you.

I think our first job on our first day as volunteer youth workers is beginning to demonstrate that, unlike other adults, we're not required to be present with kids, and our free choice to be there is a signal we don't want anything from them. Quite the opposite: We're there to serve kids—not on their terms necessarily, but certainly *in* their terms. And their terms are clearly *relational*.

When adolescents come to believe we're interested in them as people—we're there to serve them and help them grow—they'll learn to trust us and, bit by bit, become interested in what we think and believe.

THREE ESSENTIALS FOR BUILDING RELATIONSHIPS

When you enter a youth group that's already up and running, it takes a little time to find your place. Because kids are accustomed to encountering adults with some kind of agenda that depends on their time and talent (kids' time and talent I mean—in sports, piano lessons, part-time employment, growing a bigger youth group, whatever), there's a good chance you'll be greeted with mild indifference and maybe even suspicion. This can make your early experience in the group a little tougher than you might hope. But overcoming those barriers isn't rocket science. It's...forgive me if this seems too obvious: relationships. I won't pretend to unpack all that implies, but here are three relational patterns I think matter a lot to youth workers.

FAITHFULNESS

If you sign on to work with kids, then work at working with kids. Be there when you say you'll be there. Tell people what to expect from you, then follow through. If you're on a team,

4

THREE ESSENTIALS FOR BUILDING RELATIONSHIPS

When you enter a youth group that's already up and running, it takes a little time to find your place. Because kids are accustomed to encountering adults with some kind of agenda that depends on their time and talent (*kids'* time and talent, I mean—in sports, piano lessons, part-time employment, growing a bigger youth group...whatever), there's a good chance you'll be greeted with mild indifference and maybe even suspicion. This can make your early experience in the group a little tougher than you might hope. But overcoming those barriers isn't rocket science; it's...forgive me if this seems too obvious...relationships. I won't pretend to unpack all that implies, but here are three relational patterns I think matter a lot to youth workers.

FAITHFULNESS

If you sign on to work with kids, then *work* at working with kids. Be there when you say you'll be there. Tell people what to expect from you, then follow through. If you're in a team, your fellow youth workers have to know they *can* depend on you before they *will* depend on you. It's not likely you'll ever be fired from your volunteer position for poor follow-through. But if folks don't have confidence you'll deliver what you promise, they'll work around you.

What's true for your comrades in youth ministry is also true for kids and their parents. If you're not seeing your group once a week, give or take, there's very little hope of building the kind of trust that makes relationships sustainable. So, show up rain or shine, in good times and bad, season after season, where it matters to kids.

Healthy connections take time and focus. Adolescents learn appropriate self-disclosure from adults who practice appropriate self-disclosure *over time*. Kids come to trust adults who consistently ask thoughtful questions and listen carefully. Show up four weeks in a row, and kids will start expecting you to be there. Carve out a weekend to be with students at a camp or retreat, and all things being equal, they'll start treating you like someone who *gets it*.

But don't expect to see anything lasting in less than a semester—the basic unit of time in most youth ministries because it's the basic unit of time in most schools:

first semester + second semester + summer = one year.

All that said, sooner or later and from time to time you'll have scheduling conflicts. That doesn't have to be a crisis. Tell people you'll be gone on vacation or business or whatever and make an attempt to connect—if only for that week— via email or text message or some other medium to let them know you're thinking about them. If your commitment is to the midweek meeting at your church, and you know you'll be away the following week, consider adding an extra hour on Sunday morning so you can sit in on the Sunday morning youth gathering—or drop by for five minutes at the beginning or the end of the Sunday session just to touch base. Over time that kind of attention has a positive, cumulative effect.

OPENNESS

If you want kids to trust you, trust them with the truth about yourself. You have to decide what that looks like in terms of self-disclosure—what's appropriate, what's too much. I can't say I've always gotten that right. For a long time I said too little about my struggles and slowness to trust God. Then for a while I sometimes said too much (or at least sometimes gave too much detail). I got some help on this from my friends in Alcoholics Anonymous who are learning to make "a searching and fearless moral inventory" of themselves—no picnic, by the way—and then admit to God, themselves, and to another human being "the exact nature of their wrongs." Admitting the *exact nature* of our wrongs is not the same as revealing the gory details of our misbehavior to a shocked (or giggling) group of teenagers. Admitting the exact nature of our wrongs doesn't look anything like bragging about how badly we behaved or what we got away with. Figure out for yourself how to be as open as you believe you should be with your life in all its dimensions. Then find the language to express your openness with humility, personal accountability, and genuine gratitude for God's mercy.

I'm not suggesting you enlist adolescents to be your support group. I'm only saying openness from adults is so rare, kids tend to respond positively to those who present themselves as real people—with weaknesses as well as strengths and story lines that include their journeys from where they started toward a destination they have yet to reach. The typical youth-leader-who's-got-it-all-together representation is far more discouraging to kids than most of us realize.

KINDNESS

Treat adolescents the way you want to be treated.

I suppose I could end there, and we could get on with our lives. But I'll add a final flourish (assuming you'll skip ahead if you've had enough). Take a trip down memory lane and recall as much as you can about what it was like being 12, 13, 14, 15, 16, 17, 18...

- How did you feel about being teased?
- How did you feel about being listened to?
- How did you feel about being lectured?
- How did you feel about being respected?
- How did you feel about being taken seriously?
- How did you feel about your body?
- How emotionally stable were you?
- How were things with your family?
- How were your friendships?
- How did you feel about people who projected their experiences on you?
- What did you do about rivalries and adversarial relationships?
- How did your understanding of God emerge in those years?

Think about your life. Be kind. Treat kids the way you want to be treated.

5

PAYING ATTENTION TO THE WORLD AS IT IS

There's a sense in which you've been preparing to work with adolescents your whole life. You already survived being a kid, more or less intact. On one level that's almost all the preparation you need.

On another level it's worth saying that even though you were 15 once upon a time, you were never 15 exactly like *these* people are 15. By which I mean, *the game has changed.*

Teenagers are not more mature today. As they exit high school, if maturity is measured by the capacity to get out there and do what needs doing every day, many adolescents are in fact less mature than young folks of earlier generations, many of whom were trained and entrusted with more responsibility for meaningful tasks at earlier ages. This lack of meaningful roles for children and adolescents—especially since they mature physically, intellectually, and emotionally at about the same pace as the generations before them—may be one factor in the sizable population of *boomerang kids:* people who exit their families briefly, then return as legal adults to live with their parents indefinitely.[1]

Contemporary adolescents are not more mature, but they're more sophisticated than previous-generation adolescents. They see more, do more, go more, and have more at earlier ages than any generation ever. *That's* how the game has changed: because most adolescents don't know what to *do* with that accelerated experience. And neither do their parents.

This is one reason we need youth workers. But not any old youth workers. We need youth workers who pay attention to the world as it is—which is quite different from the world as it's supposed to be. When we pay attention, kids tell us and show us a lot of what they need.

We'll dip deeper into this later. For now let's start by paying attention to what kids talk about. This is the passive side of learning to listen, and all it requires is being present long enough and often enough to observe—without snooping—what kids think about life, the universe, and everything. What excites the kids you know? What makes them angry? What frightens them? What makes them think? If you listen, directly or indirectly, they'll tell you.

A great deal of field research indicates the difficulty of talking and paying attention at the same time. It follows that a key skill for youth workers is learning to keep the ears and eyes open and the mouth shut for several minutes at a stretch.

One way to accomplish this is by paying attention in settings where you have little or nothing to add. I've learned a great deal by listening to kids talk to each other in restaurants

[1] It's too much to go into here, but I addressed these dynamics at length in a book called *Raising Adults*—Google it if you like.

and food courts. And I've learned by listening quietly to the cabin chatter after the lights are out at camp, as the boys talk themselves out and fall asleep one by one. I don't always like what I hear—but I can't speak into problems and opportunities if I don't know they exist so...

Another quite potent way to pay attention takes the form of asking open-ended questions, then staying quiet except to ask for clarification. I recall a memorable hour on a bus trip when I asked everyone to describe their perfect date—from beginning to end—if they didn't have to worry about money or adult permission. It was illuminating because, having chosen to listen rather than talk for that hour, I became a student. Of course, what I learned there made its way into what I taught in the months that followed. And that's the payoff if we need one: In the act of paying attention to the world as it is, we learn what we need to know in order to teach. If we really pay attention to how kids answer our most thoughtful questions, we can establish ourselves as people to be trusted and listened to in return. Because—and you can take this to the bank—people listen to people who listen.

6

PEOPLE LISTEN TO PEOPLE WHO LISTEN

If paying attention to what kids talk about is the passive side of listening, what's the active side? Here's the script for a digital movie I wrote for DCLA and the Youth Specialties CORE tour. It's my best shot at putting words to the adolescent longing to be heard....

> Listen
> You wanna know how I'm doing?
> Don't ask.
>
> Seriously.
> Don't ask if you're not ready to listen.
> Don't say, "How you doin'?"
> I'll just say, "Fine."
> It's the answer I'm trained to give
> —whether it's true or not.
> A shallow answer
> to a shallow question.
> Most people don't really wanna know;
> they assume I know they're just being polite.

I don't think that's polite at all.
Short questions get short answers.
You wanna know how I'm doing?
Ask what I've been up to;
what I'm working on;
what's up with my family.

If you're asking me (and I sensed you were),
most of the best questions don't have question marks:
"Tell me about your sister."
"I'd like to hear about your job."
"Tell me how you felt."
"Tell me what you mean."
"I'd like to know more about that."

You wanna know how I feel when
you ask questions that way?
I feel included.
I feel cared for.
I feel like I belong.

Please...
if you already know the answer,
it's not really a question, is it...
—it's a test.
Please don't do that to me.
(I hate tests.)

Don't make me look foolish.
Don't trick me.
Don't use me to
make a point.

If you're serious,
ask what I think,
ask how I feel,
ask an honest question,
and wait for my honest answer.

Learn from silence.
If I don't answer right away
—if the silence goes on too long—
ask what that means.
Maybe I'm embarrassed.
Maybe I didn't understand the question.
(Maybe you weren't clear.)
Maybe I'm thinking (and wouldn't that be nice).
You wanna know how I'm doing?
Sometimes I'm sad
because life is confusing
and painful,
and we both know
there's nothing you can do to fix that.
It's okay. I'll be fine...truly.

That doesn't mean I don't want you to check.
Give me a chance to tell you when I'm fine,
and maybe I'll tell you when I'm not.

Don't take my first response
at face value.
Listen with your eyes:
Do I look like I'm doing all right?
Listen with your heart: Do you believe my answer?

With the very best motives
—sometimes with the worst—
I'm capable of every kind of deceit.
Just like you.
Don't ask me to do what you won't.
If you wanna know my story,
tell me yours.
Let me know I'm safe—
let me know you're not perfect either.

When I believe that,
I'll talk your ear off.

Read that with a group of adolescents, give it a moment to sink in, then ask—

- What do you think is the most significant thing in the piece?
- Why do you think that stands out for you?
- How can you imagine that making a difference if you acted on it?

If you draw those kids out and really listen to what they say, I'm betting it will make a difference in how they listen to what *you* say. Tell me if it turns out I'm wrong about that.

7

THE THREE BEST QUESTIONS I KNOW

The three best questions I know are explorations of *what, why,* and *how:*

- Talk about *what* you think is important.
- Talk about *why* you think it's important.
- Talk about *how* you think that changes things.

I like these questions because they're honest. They're not meant to persuade or challenge or compel; they're meant to clarify.

Asking *what, why,* and *how* questions is an offer to pay attention to another person's perceptions, thoughts, ideas, hopes, and intentions. If you can get honest answers to these three questions, you'll know where things stand with the other person and you'll have an idea of what to do next.

Begin with any human experience—a movie, a sermon, a song, an argument, a book, an accident, an *aha!*, a success, a failure, a passage from the Bible, a discovery...*anything* at all. Then ask, "Tell me what you think that was. What just happened?"

Don't get hung up on the wording; there's more than one way to ask *what*.

What? = What do you think happened? = What stood out for you? = Did anything surprise you? = Describe it to me. = Tell me about it...

Whatever words you use, *what* questions invite a person to describe her own perceptions of an experience. It really doesn't matter what experience; what matters is hearing her describe it (so you don't just assume, or guess, or wish).
The same is true for why questions.

Why? = So what? = Why is that significant to you? = Why do you think it happened? = Tell me more about that...

However you ask, the *why* question explores *why, out of all possible meanings, did* this *one occur to you?* The answer can tell you something you couldn't know if you didn't pose the question.

Asking *why* can be the catalyst for deeper reflection by the person on the receiving end of the question:

- Asking, "Why do you think you identified more closely with that character than the others?" invites reflection about empathy and compassion.

- Asking, "Why do you think you misunderstood that?" invites a person to consider why he heard something that wasn't said.

- Saying, "Talk about why you find that comforting" calls for self-assessment and invites self-disclosure.

And so it goes... These are all valuable considerations peo-ple—especially adolescent people—are not often encouraged to share in an emotionally safe context.

How is the money question because it clarifies what a per-son actually learned.

How? = Now what? = How do you plan to respond? = How will that make a difference? = How does that change things? = Tell me what you intend to do about that.

Kids who can answer *how* questions—especially if they follow through on their intentions to behave differently, to repeat a success, or to avoid a failure—have really learned something from their experience.

Simplicity is part of the beauty of this process. Once you learn to ask these questions naturally and unself-consciously, you can help kids understand what you're doing and why. For the last couple of decades, I've urged kids to ask these three types of questions at the end of every reading assignment and class session—promising they'll raise their grade by half a point minimum. I have yet to hear from any dissatisfied cus-tomers.

Here's why I think this works in youth ministry: I think these three questions swing the spotlight around to where it belongs—so we can see the learner. We already have a pret-ty good idea what the teacher knows; it's right there in the presentation (whatever that may be). Transferring wisdom isn't merely a matter of making statements—what passes for *teaching* most of the time. Transferring wisdom depends on engaging students where they are and helping them take the next step toward where they need to go.

I've come to believe that people learn what they *can* learn—what they're *prepared* to learn—not what they're *supposed* to learn. Good teachers don't pour knowledge into people; good teachers create intriguing environments where learners find what they need to modify or build on what they've learned so far. As a teacher the best tool I have for that task is engaging kids in new experiences (of whatever sort) and then asking *what, why,* and *how.*

8

GIVING BETTER THAN WE GOT

I grew up in church. I'm the son of a preacher. So I never missed church as a child—ever.

As a consequence, I gained a reasonable familiarity with the Bible; I learned about as much as a youngster can (and perhaps more than he should) know about church politicking; I learned the songs and hymns and jargon and customs of my family's little corner of Christendom. I did not, however, learn how unbalanced my family was.

I grew up assuming bitterness was normal. I thought angry tears and closed doors were normal. I believed it was normal to behave one way in private and another way in public. The summer I turned 14, my mother and I drove from Florida to California. About an hour into that drive she said my father wouldn't be at home when we got back. I knew things had grown progressively worse in our household, but I was taken aback. Christians—especially pastors—did not divorce in those days, not in our part of the church.

I was also more than a little relieved. My father's departure meant an end to the hostilities, an end to the awful dread I felt whenever we were all together in the house or car. I felt terribly guilty about that, but there it was: *the end of the world as we knew it (and I felt fine...sort of)*.

A long time later, my father came clean with me.

I had long known about his sexual misconduct. He got a young woman pregnant—twice in the span of a year. The first pregnancy ended in a miscarriage, which was somehow revealed to my mother and after which my father swore he'd learned his lesson. My mother found it impossible to excuse the second pregnancy. They were married 23 years.

Over time I learned all this. What I didn't know—what never occurred to me—was that my old man was a habitual offender. Had he possessed the language for it, he might have said he was a *sex addict*. What he did say, when I was 37, was he'd been unfaithful to my mother from the beginning—his actual words were, "I was never faithful to your mother."

This was stunning news from a man I remember preaching impassioned, indignant sermons about the sexual revolution and the high price of free love in the 1960s. (I guess he knew.) I felt foolish to have taken so much at face value...

On the other hand, it was in some ways a relief to hear his story. For one thing his admission struck me as evidence of the power of the gospel he preached so long and in the end really believed. Beyond all this, my father's confession put my life in perspective.

I've struggled my whole life with compulsive behaviors and the desire to control people by charm or hard work or, if nothing else worked, lies. I have been self-centered and full of pride—notwithstanding claims about the transforming presence of God's Spirit. I have sometimes been at the point of despair over my inability to overcome my hidden struggles and wrongdoing.

For a long time all that remained secret because I was too big a fake and too cowardly to make my own confession. I take full responsibility for that. At the same time I can't be the only one who's noticed how rare it is for church leaders to admit any current struggles... When I was young, I ate up that whole "From Crime To Christ!" genre of sensational self-disclosure: "come hear the startling testimony of one who murdered for fun and profit—until his own *Damascus Road* experience." I suppose that kind of spectacle inclined me to believe that the God who could do such big things might also do a little thing in my life—because didn't my shame seem little compared to the journey "From Crime To Christ"?

But of course it wasn't little. My self-centeredness might just as well have been at the center of creation's fall as Adam's or Eve's or yours.

Hearing my father's confession, I just wanted to be angry with him, but I couldn't find that in me. Instead I found myself propelled further along a course I'd already chosen—a journey on which we are all in the same boat, all living with the consciousness of the wrong things we've done and the right things we've failed to do. Most of us are afraid because our boat seems always on the verge of being swamped, and not because God fails to deal with our madness, but because we...because I...have failed to deal with it, failed to turn my back on it, walk away from it, surrender it unconditionally to the God of tender mercy "by which the rising sun will come to us from heaven" (Luke 1:78)—or, at the very least, live with it humbly the way Paul describes living with that "thorn" in my flesh (2 Corinthians 12:7-8).

Besides my slowness to get all this, what bothers me today is knowing I was well into my 30s before I really heard anyone speaking plainly about these things in the church. Like my father before me, I announced grace and mercy from Christ, all the while knowing—but not saying—how uncomfortably that grace and mercy fit me. The conversation must have been going on long before I joined it—it must have; but it must have been in another room in the house...

Of course you know, more or less, how this story plays out. I came to see that, though we didn't speak of it in the churches I was part of, this pilgrimage of broken people was not strange ground to God's people at the church's beginnings. It's mostly sugarcoated in the sermons I've heard, but there it is, clear as day in Romans 7, 2 Corinthians 12, James 5, 1 John 1...and most of the Psalms and Ecclesiastes and the other writings...the Law of Moses and all the Prophets and every book of history from Joshua to the Acts of the Apostles—in other words...*everywhere*.

There's much more to be said about all this, but for now I've said this much in order to say one particular thing about youth work: I think Christians really should know all this before they get into their 30s. And if people like us come clean about our own brokenness, they can; they can guess how much they're going to need grace and mercy for the rest of their lives by listening to our true and humble stories of needing and receiving grace and mercy ourselves. Sure that means being a little bit vulnerable, and it means wondering if we'll be the first volunteers ever fired from youth ministry for telling the truth.

My story is, once I started coming clean, I didn't get fired from my job as a professional youth worker, and I didn't get fired as a volunteer. And, in fact, people have seemed more likely than ever to seek me out in the face of trouble.

How that feels on the inside is mainly good. I feel vulnerable sometimes, but mostly I feel free. Being willing to admit the worst stuff about me, I no longer worry about being found out.

I admit I've stepped over the line of good taste occasionally—telling people more than they wanted or needed to know—and I feel sorry about that. But I think I'm learning how to speak the truth in love—what I think James was getting at when he said, "...confess your sins to each other and pray for each other so that you may be healed" (James 5:16).

You have to decide how much of a fellow pilgrim you're going to be with kids and other youth workers—how straight you believe you should tell it and how straight you're willing to tell it. Start with an inventory. Answer this question as honestly and thoroughly as you can: *what is it about you that lets you know you need God's grace right now—not five or 10 or 20 years ago but right* now?

Take your time. Get alone with a clean sheet of paper and a couple of number two pencils and start writing. Don't stop with the obvious. Keep reminding yourself the bad news isn't nearly as bad as the Good News is good.

I think we owe our young friends a clearer description of what it means to be Christians than some of us got when we were growing up. If you're already doing that, please accept my appreciation and carry on. In this one way, at least, we get to influence what happens in the next generation of people who follow Jesus. I don't think anyone meant to do us any harm (they were only doing what they were taught), but harm's been done nonetheless. I think we have to give better than we got.

9

INCARNATION: BEING THERE

"She is grace incarnate," folks say of a wonderful dancer or athlete; "he is the incarnation of evil," people say—and usually not in the positive sense. *Incarnation* means being present in flesh and blood.

The amateur youth worker doesn't volunteer because it's fun (though it often is). She does it to give the gospel a flesh and blood presence among kids—to make the gospel *incarnate* by her life—because she's convinced that is the only way it works. If she isn't present with kids in their world, she may as well post a blog and hope young readers stumble across it as they navigate the Internet in search of meaning.

For my money, incarnation is the first and biggest idea in youth ministry—any ministry really. John, whose Gospel came decades after Matthew, Mark, and Luke, had plenty of time to think about where to begin. He chose to lead his telling of the story with a brief theology of incarnation that comes to a white-hot point in the line:

"The Word became flesh and made his dwelling among us" (John 1:14).

As far as I'm concerned, this notion that the coming of Jesus Christ is nothing less than God's radical identification with humankind—without which we would be wonderful creatures but not the Creator's adopted daughters and sons—this is the notion that sets Christian faith apart from everything else.

Everything else seems to be about pursuing and finding God; Christian faith is about being pursued and found by God. The New Testament book Hebrews describes how God regards humankind, saying: "Jesus is not ashamed to call them brothers and sisters," and, "Since the children have flesh and blood, he too shared in their humanity..." (2:11, 14).

Paul picked up this thread in the third and fourth chapters of Galatians, arguing that the law was a substitute teacher until the coming of Christ: "But when the set time had fully come, God sent his Son, born of a woman, born under the law, to redeem those under the law, that we might receive adoption to sonship" (4:4-5).

Experts and authors may be comfortable telling kids what to believe and how to behave. *Amateurs* wade in, bearing witness to God's relentless love by entering into the lives of adolescents. As good ol' boy Texas Bix Bender is reputed to have said, "A body can pretend to care, but he cannot pretend to be there." Nothing says "You matter" like showing up.

People like you, who volunteer to represent Christ to kids, cast a dim shadow of God's grand miracle of incarnation. You're already human, so the distance you seek to span isn't inconceivable (you're even a former teenager, so you've got that going for you). But you're an *adult* human, and if we've learned anything about big people it's the blinding speed with which most adults forget what it's like to be young (and never look back if they can help it).

Thanks for not being that guy. Thanks for doing what C. S. Lewis celebrated when he wrote about the very positive act of stooping to the place where "adult minds (but only the best of them) can descend into sympathy with children."[2] Thanks for volunteering to go back in time to a place of vulnerability and uncertainty, for shelving some of what you know about life to remember and identify with the agony and glory of adolescents. If you keep after it, kids will notice, and some of them will respond to you. You will embody the difference between those who talk *about* kids or *at* them and those who, like you, talk *with* kids. Because you're there, they'll *get it*.

[2] C. S. Lewis, *Miracles* (New York: Macmillan, 1947), 111.

10

GOING WHERE KIDS ARE
(OR WOULD LIKE TO BE)

If the story of God's incarnation in Jesus Christ is true, I take it as the ultimate proof of God's choice to do whatever it takes to reach humankind with what is certainly the best news I can imagine. In that frame, all God's games are played on the road—they're all *away* games. I think that's remarkable. It's what Karl Barth was talking about when he argued that "In his Son he is completely himself and completely for us and with us," not against us.[3] Looking at Jesus, I have a hard time denying that God goes the extra mile.

I think there's a model for youth ministry in that concept: effective youth workers don't simply invite kids to come where adults are and then hope someone shows up. Literally and figuratively, effective youth workers go where kids are.

That begins with paying attention to what matters to adolescents in general and then translates into acts of intentional engagement with individual kids. The next step takes adults beyond the safe zone to go where kids are—venturing onto

---

[3] Karl Barth, *God Here and Now* (New York: Routledge Classics, 2003), 15

middle school and senior high campuses for plays, practices, sporting events, exhibitions, and concerts. The gift you give a ninth grader when you show up for a JV basketball game is immeasurable. Show up for a high school forensics meet, and they'll try to make you a saint.

Going where kids are is matched by finding appropriate ways to take them where they'd like to go but can't without adult supervision. I'm not talking about R-rated movies; I'm talking about Friday night laser shows at the planetarium (there aren't many parents willing to stay up late for that one). And I'm talking about bike rides and day hikes and overnight camping adventures, about holiday shopping excursions, museums and zoos, picnics, carefully chosen all-ages rock and pop and hip-hop and jazz shows, beaches, ski trips, amusement parks, novelty restaurants, and service projects. Every time I've done one of those things with a group of kids, it's been interpreted by them and by their parents as an act of love. I can't say I enjoyed every one of those experiences for its own sake, but I don't recall ever resenting or regretting the time I shared with kids.

And that's just me. I know youth workers who take kids fishing, skating, snowboarding, surfing, and target shooting; teach kids photography, sound, lighting, video production, baking, quilting; youth workers who become assistant coaches; direct school plays and musical events; fly model airplanes with kids; tutor kids in math, reading, and writing... Effective youth workers leverage what *they're* good at; what they enjoy; their passions, gifts, and hobbies to engage kids who are discovering what they're good at, what they enjoy and feel passionate about.

Forging wholesome connections with adolescents isn't that difficult. Figure out where kids are—or want to be—and go there with them.

THE MOUNTAINTOP: TAKING KIDS TO CAMP

Taking kids to a camp or conference can be great fun, and it can just as certainly be a big pain in the rear. It's a weekend (or more) out of your life with too little sleep, too much stimulation, and more responsibility for the health and safety of other people's children than most adults want to take. Taking kids to camp is totally worth it.

I'm one of a thousand or more old youth workers who claim to have been the first to say, "We accomplish more in a weekend at camp than we do in six months of normal youth ministry at home." (Were my mother still alive, she'd confirm those were my first words at the age of 16 months—after which I was silent until age seven. Seriously...why would I lie about something like this?)

Camps and retreats can produce amazing results for kids, individually and in groups. Being away together—living in close proximity, even for a couple of nights—breaks down barriers and forges bonds between kids and leaders. Everybody sees everybody else in their underwear, and nobody cares (okay, don't go all literal on me; I'm just trying to make a point). Camp is—or can be—a moratorium from ordinary living, a setting aside of normal routines to pay attention to God and each other. We get to have long, uninterrupted conversations about things that matter. Boys rediscover the joys of breaking wind in the moments after lights out. Girls do whatever it is girls do when they're together (I've heard stories and rumors too fantastical to be true). We establish traditions together. Kids feel accepted (if we take pains to create safety). Some kids save up problems and bring them to camp, hoping for solutions and the experience of God's forgiveness. Lots and lots of kids put their trust in Jesus at camp. Camp is *great!*

Except when it isn't.

Camp isn't great for everyone. Some people get emotionally and relationally killed at camp. For some reason their underwear *does* matter, and other kids give them a hard time about very personal and private things. Some kids don't *go* to camp; they are *sent* to camp by parents who are hoping for a reboot without their having to do anything but write a check.

And some kids are sent to camp "because it will be good for them." One of the finest things I ever saw in youth work happened at a junior high camp where Dave, an amateur whose day job was computer engineering, spent the entire week in a wheelchair or scooting around the floor on his knees or bottom. Dave did this so his young friend Robbie wouldn't be the only person at camp in a wheelchair. Dave did everything Robbie did. He showered in his chair. He balanced on his knees to play volleyball, just like Robbie. (Robbie's whole team assumed that posture, and after a point or two, so did the other team.) Dave wasn't showing off. He was making it possible for a seventh grader in a wheelchair to see eye to eye with at least one other person. Dave made junior high camp safe—he helped Robbie turn a week of camp he dreaded beforehand into a week he loved.

That's why someone like *you*—who loves and protects and nurtures kids—must be the one who takes them to camp. Because you're the sort of person who will make camp a safe, inviting, engaging place to know and be known, to listen and be heard, to relax and play and reflect and just *be*. I don't know how else to get that big a block of uninterrupted time to pay attention to kids. So yes, my life is busy, but when camp comes around, sign me up—it'll be totally worth it.

12

THE LETDOWN: WHEN WHAT HAPPENS AT CAMP STAYS AT CAMP

I really like the story in the gospel of John often referred to as "The Woman at the Well." I like it for a lot of reasons, but today I like it because of what it says about the townspeople that woman led out to meet Jesus after his unsettling conversation with her. Here it is in *The Message:*

> Many of the Samaritans from that village committed themselves to him because of the woman's witness: "He knew all about the things I did. He knows me inside and out!"
>
> They asked him to stay on, so Jesus stayed two days. A lot more people entrusted their lives to him when they heard what he had to say. They said to the woman, "We're no longer taking this on your say-so. We've heard it for ourselves and know it for sure. He's the Savior of the world!" (John 4:39-42)

"We've heard it for ourselves and know it for sure." I love the clarity of that. It sounds like something you hear on the last night at camp. Bam! Two days with Jesus and we get it!

However, I've *been* to camp, and I have to wonder if those Samaritans still held onto that clarity two months later. Or did they experience the sort of spiritual chaos the rest of us live with—especially when we're adolescents: We're up, we're down; we're turned on, we're turned off; we're on fire, we're burned out. We go to camp and—bam! We get it! Then we're shocked because sometimes what happens at camp stays at camp.

This is why adolescents need adult leaders in their lives. Not because adults are better—Lord knows—just farther along the road, more experienced in coping with spiritual ups and downs.

Some of the tears kids shed as camp ends are informed by their having been there before, too: raised to the heights and then brought low because...well, there are a lot of reasons, so let's say *just because*.

A long time ago there was a wonderful story in *Campus Life* magazine called "The Red Chair Incident" or something like that. In this story a girl goes to camp and has a breathtaking encounter with God, which she hopes with all her heart will change everything. But she knows she has to go home where much sooner than later she'll come into conflict with her sister over the red chair planted on prime real estate in front of the television set. That red chair is emblematic of everything selfish and competitive between the two sisters. And when the girl thinks about all that, she's sickened by fear the red chair will prove that, really, nothing has changed. And wouldn't it be nice just to stay at camp and never have to face the past? A lot of people have wished that...

You can reduce the negative effects of post-camp letdown by addressing it in generous and realistic terms while you're on the mountaintop and again after you come back down to earth:

- Make a point of connecting with kids who had significant experiences at camp in the week or so after.

- Ask them "the three best questions" from chapter six.

- Affirm that spiritual growth—like all growth—is a process and support that with honest recollections from your own life.

- Organize a camp reunion a few weeks after the experience to tell stories and encourage each other.

- Support the notion that a post-camp letdown doesn't mean what happened on the mountaintop wasn't real— it may simply mean the experience wasn't meant to last in that form; it was meant to energize life back where we live. Here's a bit of prose from the French writer René Daumal that might help you make that point:

> You cannot stay on the summit forever; you have to come down again...so why bother in the first place? Just this: What is above knows what is below, but what is below does not know what is above.... One climbs, one sees, one descends. One sees no longer but one has seen. There is an art of conducting oneself in the lower regions by the memory of what one saw higher up. When one can no longer see, one can at least still know.[4]

[4] René Daumal, *Mount Analogue* (Woodstock, NY: Overlook, 1952), 153.

Like the Samaritan villagers in "The Woman at the Well" story, growing adolescents are in a process of shifting from a spiritual understanding that's *received* to an understanding that's *believed*. Which means cultivating a habit of calling to mind in the valley what they saw from the mountaintop.

The girl in "The Red Chair" found out how real her experience on the mountaintop was when her sister, ignoring a clear "seat saved" call, snaked the chair while the girl was out of the room. Finding her sister sprawled on the red chair when she returned, something happened inside her that freaked both of them out a little. Ignoring the flagrant "seat saved" violation, she crossed the room and took another seat because the red chair no longer meant the same thing to her; for the first time, it was just a chair. That was a turning point for her—the day she knew she was changing from the inside out. It was also a turning point for her sister who had to take seriously the possibility this alleged encounter with God might be a real deal—because how else could she account for the red chair incident?

13

CROSSING CULTURES (SORT OF)

Youth ministry is a cross-cultural mission...sort of. Yes, we share a common mother tongue, but the overlap of social and cultural space is far less than 100 percent. So it's as significant an adjustment for many adults to enter "kid world" as it is for adolescents making their way in what big people like to refer to as "the real world." At its best, kid world is an engaging, entertaining place for adults—at its worst it can be disorienting, offensive, threatening, shocking.

It's important to hear what kids say; it's almost as important—from time to time at least—to hear what kids *hear*. Hearing what kids hear doesn't take much effort. Tune your radio, at least occasionally, to stations people in your group listen to.

The same is true for seeing what kids *see*. Watch some television shows and movies you hear kids talk about. Visit some Web sites frequented by adolescents. Scan a few magazines that cater to teen audiences.

Undertake this as a learner, not so you can store up ammunition for an assault against them. Remember that only a fraction of what you see and hear in these media was created by kids; most of it was designed "for" kids by adults doing their best to get something (mostly money) in return.

When and if the time comes to talk about why kids pay attention to some of the stranger voices directed at them, you'll be more persuasive by far in a straight-across discussion—which by definition is 50 percent listening—than if you decide to make proclamations from on high (especially if those proclamations spring from hostility, hearsay, or surface impressions).

And remember Rule One in crossing cultures: Never confuse *different* with *bad*.

14
YOUTH CULTURE SHOCK

Wave on wave of hormone-drenched bodies,
fruity potions, spritzed and slathered musk,
pungent whiff of sweaty shirts and hair,
and the racket in sheer decibels would be enough,
but this high-frequency squeal:
Can it be human?
(No wonder dogs howl all down the block—
they must be writhing in pain;
their ears must be bleeding.)
WAIT! *Shh!*
What is that silence?
We are saved by the bell—
fourth period has begun.

If you've been away long enough to forget the sensory overload, your first new contact with a herd of adolescents may be...overwhelming. If you find your nose twitching, your head spinning, take a moment; get your bearings; remember who you are and where you came from. Decide—and it *is* a decision—really to see what you're seeing, because the first hint of culture shock is difficulty seeing what's right in front of us.

Youth culture shock—like culture shock in its more familiar forms—is an experience of disorientation. Maybe you've experienced this in a foreign country. The sights and sounds and smells, even the textures, are confusing; the air seems harsh; everything looks shabby. You find yourself wondering what's wrong with these people.

There's probably *nothing* wrong with these people. Perhaps they're poor, but that's no crime; maybe they're just different. People in the grip of culture shock have trouble with that. They're tempted to withdraw to overly simple—almost always mistaken—explanations of what they're seeing, hearing, smelling, tasting, touching, and feeling.

Youth culture shock strikes people this way, too. Nothing's wrong with kids; they're just different, just...*young*.

A kid in pain may only seem like trouble to an adult suffering youth culture shock. A grown-up may fail to see that an adolescent who appears sullen, aloof, or uncommunicative is actually paralyzed by profound shyness or shame or self-doubt.

Youth culture shock—like other culture shock—is unpredictable. It happens when it happens. You turn a corner and find yourself unexpectedly put off by a circle of ninth-grade girls—even though you have nieces the same age and think they're great. You feel antagonism toward a kid whose cease-less attachment to his iPod/Game Boy/PSP/media player and earbuds strikes you as willful, flagrant rudeness—even if, in the rest of your life, you exhibit a similar umbilical relationship to your iPhone/BlackBerry/Palm/personal digital device. Youth culture shock isn't rational; it's emotional.

People suffering youth culture shock may become overly emotional, reacting strongly to things that wouldn't ordinarily set them off. They may deflect what they're feeling into inappropriate emotional expressions such as sarcasm or lashing out. They may go inside with their emotions and get very quiet. They may display addictive behaviors like compulsive overeating, starving, drinking, acting out sexually, fingernail chewing, attempting to control others—the bad reaction may not come out as something specifically related to kids. I don't think anyone ever died from youth culture shock, but I've seen people go further into addictive behaviors or further away from the people they came to help. Seriously, youth ministry can mess you up if you get snared by unacknowledged youth culture shock. So if you think you see it, don't ignore it—in yourself or anyone else. That said, don't think experiencing youth culture shock means you shouldn't be a youth worker.

The cure for youth culture shock includes—

- Self-assessment: What's going on inside me? Why is this happening? How should I respond?
- Reality checks: What can other reasonable people add to my perceptions?
- Human contact: Which individual adolescents can I connect with on an appropriate personal level?

- God's-eye view: What do I know about God's attitude toward these people in general and each of them in particular?
- Prayer: God, what do you want me to do about relating to these folks?
- Perseverance: Can I stick this out awhile longer to see if my perceptions become more positive?

We have nothing to fear from youth culture shock. Lots of people survive the experience and go on to be excellent youth workers—far better than they would've been had it all come naturally and without reflection.

One thing that doesn't cure youth culture shock is retreating into privacy or a circle of adults and critiquing kids for being young. This is roughly equivalent to tourists who retire to the hotel bar and complain to other tourists about "the locals."

15

WHEN WHAT YOU HEAR SOUNDS LIKE TROUBLE

When you know how to listen to adolescents, sooner or later you'll hear things that make you sad and maybe even frighten you. Don't be shocked when it happens. Keep listening. Assume you're the right person, in the right place, at the right time. Otherwise, someone else would be there.

Is what you're hearing a drama or a crisis? You can tell an adolescent is in genuine crisis when he has trouble functioning in ordinary, day-to-day situations. Kids in crisis have trouble sleeping—or sleep too much...can't eat—or can't stop eating...can't feel—or have their emotions stuck wide-open...can't make decisions—or act impulsively.

Crises come in too many shapes and sizes to cover here. Rich Van Pelt and I wrote *The Youth Worker's Guide to Helping Teenagers in Crisis* and *The Parent's Guide to Helping Teenagers in Crisis* as field guides for understanding, preventing, and responding to crisis. The books are built around action plans for two dozen common crisis scenarios. Get a copy for yourself and another for the person you report to (and let it be known you'll be calling for help when the time comes).

While you're waiting for your *Crisis* books to arrive, there are three things I think you should know if you believe a kid is in crisis—no matter what.

1. Listen intently until she's convinced you understand and are prepared to act in her best interest. (The *Crisis* books go into considerable detail on how to listen deeply under crisis conditions...and that's my next- to-last commercial plug.)

2. Once she's convinced you've heard her—unless you believe it will create real danger (as distinct from mere embarrassment)—help her involve her parents. This will help them account for side effects such as a temporary drop in grades or crisis-induced fatigue.

3. Introduce her to someone who can offer more help than you, taking pains to make it clear you're *adding* another, even more competent helper, not *subtracting* your help.

And if you believe it's *really* urgent? If you believe an adolescent is a danger to himself or others and you're also convinced his parents are a threat to his well-being, here's how to get help.

Begin by telling your boss or the head of staff in your organization, explaining what makes you think the adolescent is in danger. Things like—

- trouble functioning in ordinary, day-to-day situations
- unusual trouble sleeping—or sleeping too much
- chronic loss of appetite—or chronic binge eating

- chronic emotional flatness—or disruptive emotionalism

- inability to make decisions—or uncharacteristically impulsive behavior

- chronic and unprecedented disregard for personal well-being—or intentional self-injury

- unrelenting anger and inability to move beyond a self-defined loss

- declarations of hopelessness, self-loathing, homicidal or suicidal intent

If your staff leader seems confused or you fear he will sweep it under the rug—and you're convinced the crisis is real—take the next steps.

- Call the head counselor or vice principal at your local school. Explain who you are and how you know the student, describe why you think the student may be a danger to himself or others. There's every reason to assume this person will take it from there. She's almost certainly been down this road before, and she'll make sure things are done properly. If you don't see that happening and continue to believe the student is a danger to himself or others, take the next step.

- Call or visit the sheriff, police, or Child Protective Services (whatever it may be called where you live—law enforcement jurisdictions can be confusing, so keep after it, humbly and persistently).

- If all else fails, and you believe a kid is an immediate danger to himself or others, dial 911 and explain the threat in calm, clear language.

The threshold in each of these scenarios is your reasonable conviction of danger to life and limb—and that's a judgment call. One way or another you have to live with your decision. So listen, think, breathe, pray, and ask for help until you get it. Be humble but unwavering—like the widow in the story Jesus told who came seeking justice day after day until the judge paid attention (Luke 18:1-8). Don't showboat, but don't give up.

Full disclosure: I learned most of these things while I was a professional youth worker. But I've done most of them as a post-professional amateur living in towns where I had to start from scratch to find help for kids in crisis. I'm pretty sure there's nothing here you can't do in a pinch—especially if you resist the urge to go all cowboy on the problem. Just begin at the top of the list and work your way down...

16

REPORTING ABUSE

You have to do it.

As a volunteer youth worker you're almost certainly required by law to report any act you believe a reasonable person would call child abuse.[5] Here are the criteria for making that call:

- *Physical abuse* is any maltreatment that causes or could cause physical injury to a child.[6]

- The law defines *child* as anyone under the age of 18.

- The law defines *child sexual abuse* as inappropriate adolescent or adult sexual behavior with a child. It includes fondling a child's genitals, making the child fondle the older person's genitals, intercourse, incest, rape, sodomy, exhibitionism, sexual exploitation, or exposure to pornography.[7]

---

[5] I say "almost certainly" because at this writing there are a few jurisdictions where that may not be the case—but those gaps are closing rapidly, so it's best to assume you are a *mandated reporter*.

[6] U.S. Department of Health and Human Services, Administration on Children, Youth and Families, *Child Maltreatment 2002* (Washington, D.C.: U.S. Government Printing Office, 2004), 100.

[7] Ibid, Appendix B. The law makes allowances for some consensual sexual contact between adolescent peers—but the same contact between an adolescent and a younger child is defined as sexual abuse.

If you have reason to believe any of these acts has occurred, assume you have a legal obligation to report it—it's not your decision; you're obeying the law. Sometimes youth workers have let things pass—or tried to deal with things themselves—and gotten kids hurt worse than they were already. The laws are so clear-cut because everyone finally got the idea children are sitting ducks for angry and predatory adults. We mustn't overlook or excuse child abuse of any sort—it's our obligation to protect children and get crime victims to safety.

As always, if there's an immediate threat, call law enforcement without hesitation.

If there's no immediate threat, dialing 911 is probably not your best course of action. Unfortunately, what *is* the best course may not be as obvious as it should be. In some communities it's easier to find a number for dead animal disposal than child abuse reporting. Then after you find the number, you may be dialing an agency only open for business from 8 a.m. to 5 p.m., Monday through Friday. The person who answers may tell you if it's an emergency, you should dial 911; otherwise he or she will be happy to take your number, and someone will get back with you as soon as possible. Yikes!

That's why I bring it up now. You, or whoever is in charge, can make a few phone calls this week, before you need speedy access to the magic number. (HINT: The administrators at your local high school or middle school will certainly have this information.) In some instances, once they know who you are and what you're trying to do to serve kids, people responsible for child welfare will give you their direct lines.

Once you know your adolescent friend is getting the protection he needs, do this:

- Stay close to the victimized person (without hovering). Recounting the details of an abusive event or relationship would be an ordeal for almost anyone. The good news is many communities have multidisciplinary intervention teams in place to reduce the trauma kids suffer in the aftermath of crimes against them. Where this is the case, a victim is spared the agony of telling and retelling her horror story to a parade of strangers. There are a couple of reasons this isn't the last word on that: 1) There may be no intervention teams operating where you live, and 2) telling their stories to safe people can be a significant part of recovery for abused kids. So do your best to be a safe person and remain close for as long as it takes.

- Be alert for signs of self-injurious behavior. Once they've told someone about abuse, it isn't unusual for young folks to go through periods of heightened risk for self-destructive behaviors such as cutting, drug abuse, and suicide. Families don't always respond the way we hope, leaving the children unsupported. Step into the gap with God's love, comfort, assurance, and ongoing support.

- Respect people's dignity. Don't air other people's dirty laundry under the cover of a "prayer request."

- Don't feed off the emotions associated with helping in a crisis; don't let pride get the best of you; don't let it be about you—even, maybe *especially*—to you...

17

GOING TO THE HOSPITAL

You don't have to be an expert to get hospital visits right; it's mainly about being courteously attentive and keeping it short.

- Stay about one minute for every day the patient has been hospitalized. Sick and injured people don't have a lot of energy to spare, and they shouldn't have to expend it entertaining visitors—which is exactly what many people feel compelled to do for friends who show up in their hospital rooms. Give the patient a break; head for the door and let *him* tell *you* if he wants you to stay longer (that said, pay attention to subtle and indirect requests for you to stick around for a while).

- If someone else arrives to visit, excuse yourself as soon as you can do so naturally—if your friend wants you to stay, she'll let you know.

- Observe visiting hours.

- If the patient is asleep, leave a brief note. She'll be glad you were there (and relieved you didn't wake her up).

- Flowers are completely optional. If you want to show up with a gift, consider something offbeat like a coloring book and a box of crayons. It's probably better if you don't show up with a double cheeseburger.

- In general don't hug—it's awkward. Most of the time, a light touch on the forearm or a gentle squeeze of the hand is about right.

- Keep the noise down.

- Don't sit on the bed—hospital beds are narrow and the sheets don't stay tucked in. And there may be tubes and wires, and your friend probably feels underdressed and...just don't sit on the bed.

- If you see something you think is dangerous, tell a nurse. If you don't think you're being heard, tell the patient's family what you think is wrong.

- Before you leave, if you can do it naturally, ask, "Can I pray for you?" Keep it simple, short, and humble. Touch his arm or hand while you pray.

- Just be yourself. If you pretend to be someone you're not, it will ring false—so don't even try (unless you're a knucklehead, in which case acting like a normal human being for a few minutes isn't a bad thing).

18

WHEN SOMEONE DIES

When a kid loses a family member or friend, your simple presence at the residence, funeral home, church, or cemetery can be a big deal to him. And showing up may be all that's required because just being there will continue speaking long after any words you say have faded on the wind. In fact, your silent presence may be what a grieving person needs most.

Read the situation. If your young friend seems inclined to tell stories, listen intently and ask appropriate questions. If he laughs, laugh with him; if he cries, put your hand on his forearm and let him cry. Whatever you do, please resist the temptation to "solve" a person's grief with easy answers and moralizing. Grief is good—not easy or pleasant—but necessary and healthy.

Review the stages of grief identified by Elizabeth Kübler-Ross[8] so you don't try to talk a grieving kid out of feeling what she's feeling (or into feeling something she's not feeling) in the moment:

[8] *On Death and Dying* (New York: Touchstone, 1969).

- Denial. Denial—expressed by statements such as, "I can't believe she's gone" or, "This isn't happening" or by behaviors that deflect the impact of loss—is a common early response to death. Funerals and memorial services go a long way toward cementing the realization that it's really happened.

- Anger. People express anger about being abandoned; anger at the one who caused or failed to prevent a premature death, self-directed anger, anger at the dead person, anger at God. Listen to the anger—vocalizing fury is much safer than driving fast, punching walls, trashing the house, or holding it in.

- Bargaining. Attempting to bargain with God, with a parent, or with himself is a distraught person's reiteration of denial. *Knowing* the person is gone doesn't factor into the desperate offer, "I'll do *anything*, God—just please don't let this have happened." Knowing it's already happened merely haunts the grieving person.

- Depression. Emotional numbness can give way to situational depression as the weight of loss sinks in. (Here's where active listening in the form of drawing out stories and reflections about the relationship between a grieving person and the one she's lost can be a very great service.)

- Resolution. Resolution happens when it happens and not a minute sooner. The grieving person will always feel a hole where the lost friend or family member is supposed to be, but bit by bit, living with the absence becomes feasible.

Being present the first 24 hours after a loss is significant; attending the funeral or memorial service is significant. What's easy to miss is the significance of checking in a week later, and a month after, and on birthdays and holidays and important dates for the first year. Checking in is as simple as a message in any medium saying, "I'm thinking about you today, wondering how you're holding up—and praying for you." Don't do these things to *fix* a grieving person; do them as acts of service in which you come alongside to love and listen and be *with* someone who matters. The testimony of a great many people acquainted with grief confirms that the people who help most generally say the least. It's their presence that makes a difference.

19

ONE-TO-ONE
OR A SMALL GROUP?

You have to figure out for yourself when it's best to spend time with individual students and when it's more useful to engage with small groups of kids. Of course it's possible the decision has been made *for* you since, for painfully obvious reasons, some organizations have policies restricting one-to-one meetings between adults and students.

Be that as it may, count me on the list of those who think relating to kids in small affinity groups—collections of people who get along naturally because they share common ground—is often more useful than focusing on individuals anyway. I think this because, given the amount of time adolescents spend looking after each other at school and home and in the neighborhood (the attention youth workers are able to offer is a drop in the bucket compared to that ocean), they can and often do help each other in ways we can only watch and admire. I see every reason to encourage and facilitate that. Besides which—for what it's worth—a reading of the Gospels suggests Jesus spent a lot more time with people in twos and threes and dozens than one-to-one (and far more time with his small group than relating to big crowds—go back and read the text with this in mind; see if you agree).

Looking around a youth group, it doesn't take long to see who's naturally attached to whom and in what kind of relationship. Where there's a natural, reasonably healthy affinity between kids, just go with it. Building rapport with them as a group is way easier than overcoming the awkwardness that's typical at the beginning between one adult and one adolescent.

After you've been in a group for a while, it doesn't take much to help people form alliances that transcend natural connections. I once gathered a particularly interesting collection of boys for a weekly group because they all had a self-identified *life-controlling problem*—drugs, rage, sexual compulsiveness, people-pleasing, lying... These people would never have found each other at school or in the large youth group they were part of—they were just too different, coming from too many different friendship groups—but they gravitated toward the subject matter and then bonded with each other because of their mutual need for support.

I learned to think about affinity groups from reading about Jesus. If the Gospels can be trusted as reasonably accurate accounts of his associations, Jesus appears to have built on sibling relationships and other natural groupings among his friends and followers. Over time he drew diverse people together, connecting them to each other by connecting with them himself. Even when the group of close followers grew to 72 and then 120, he still seems to have related most directly to the first 12—perhaps even delegating responsibility for them to guide the development of those who came later.[9]

That strikes me as a decent model. Studying the Bible or discussing some other book or topic is generally more fruitful with two or three or a handful of kids than with just one. The same is true of teaching a skill or just hanging out.

This isn't to say you should never have conversations with just one kid (assuming your organization permits it). I've had some great and memorable experiences in one-to-one conversations. Sometimes things happen in a quiet conversation that would be very difficult to duplicate in even an intimate and trusting small group. Usually, for me, the private conversations have come second, and I encourage you to believe kids in your group will let you know if they need private time with you. They just have to believe it's okay to ask for a solo conversation. And you have to know the circumstances under which that's okay.

---

[9] Read about this for yourself. I think the relational patterns of Jesus are most apparent in Matthew, Mark, and Luke; John chimes in with a less sequential overview. If you're interested in pursuing this idea, get a copy of A. T. Robertson's classic *A Harmony of the Gospels* (San Francisco: HarperOne, 1932) in which he lays all the gospels side by side in as near chronological order as he can. It's a good, very different, reading of the narratives about Jesus.

HOW TO HAVE PRIVATE CONVERSATIONS

his won't take long.

If you're going to have a private conversation with someone who is by legal definition a child (meaning he or she is under the age of 18—though common sense tells us we're responsible for our behavior toward young men and women older than 18 if we're in positions of leadership)—confine the conversation to public spaces such as restaurants (but not cozy ones), public libraries, common areas on your church campus...always in plain sight. If you talk quietly there's little chance others will overhear what you say. If you think someone is eavesdropping, say you're having a private discussion and ask them to give you a little more space. If necessary, move to another table or bench.

If you begin a private conversation in, say, the auditorium or the youth room at your church and suddenly realize the place has emptied of all but you two, call time out long

20

HOW TO HAVE
PRIVATE
CONVERSATIONS

This won't take long.

If you're going to have a private conversation with someone who is by legal definition a child (meaning he or she is under the age of 18—though common sense tells us we're responsible for our behavior toward young men and women older than 18 if we're in positions of leadership)—confine the conversation to public spaces such as restaurants (but not cozy ones), public libraries, common areas on your church campus...*always* in plain sight. If you talk quietly, there's little chance others will overhear what you say. If you think someone is eavesdropping, say you're having a private discussion and ask them to give you a little more space. If necessary, move to another table or bench.

If you begin a private conversation in, say, the auditorium or the youth room at your church and suddenly realize the place has emptied of all but you two, call time out long enough to move to a place where you will be in the open. You don't have to make a big deal about it; you just have to do it.

All this goes double if you have even the subtlest feeling of attraction toward the younger person or sense he may be even the tiniest bit attracted to you.

I think the common sense of this is unassailable. But my father didn't—at least not until he got caught with his pants down. The only Bible verse I remember him quoting after that is 1 Corinthians 10:12 in the New American Standard Bible: "Therefore let him who thinks he stands take heed that he does not fall." Years later I read a sentence further in the text: "No temptation has overtaken you but such as is common to man; and God is faithful, who will not allow you to be tempted beyond what you are able, but with the temptation will provide the way of escape also, so that you will be able to endure it" (13). Put those two ideas together, and you can see why I try to restrict private conversations to public places.

21

LONERS AND LONELY HEARTS

It doesn't take a sociologist to spot the loners and lonely kids at the margins of a youth group. But engaging them in the life of your group begins with finding out why they're alone.

LONERS

Generally speaking—and this really is a generalization—*loner* status can be subdivided into three groups: *introverts, outsiders,* and *rejects.*

Introverts

Going to youth group—especially a group they define as large—can be hard on introverts because they tend to be drained by the sort of superficial contact that dominates a lot of youth gatherings. Challenging introverts to "go deep" doesn't help because the context is all wrong. Introverts don't want to go deep with people unless they trust them. Directions such as, "Get into pairs with someone you don't know and share a significant childhood memory—you'll each have 30 seconds…GO!" are not even a little bit inviting to introverts. In fact, they're insulting and possibly threatening. Make it your business to create safety for the introverts (who have at least as much to offer as their noisy, socially extroverted classmates). Go stand with them at the edge of the room during silly games; let them know being introverts doesn't mean they're alone.

Outsiders

Kids who live in self-imposed isolation do so for personal, often painful, reasons. Look past the barriers they erect—the clothes, the hair, the ink, the attitude, the anger, the tribalism, the foul language, the tobacco…whatever—and try to engage outsiders as human beings with strengths and weaknesses, joys and sorrows, hopes and fears. Which is exactly what they are. This sort of isolation is sometimes an invitation to take notice. No one puts tattoos on their body and then says, "What are *you* looking at?"—unless they think you're just being rude. Ditto with elaborate costumes. (I'm thinking about old-school punk, majorly oversized hip-hop, super-scruffy skate, defiantly thrift shop, and yee-haw cowboy costumes; these don't just fall off the racks down at the Target where I buy my clothes or the Nordstrom where you buy yours—or the Nordstrom Rack where we sometimes bump into each other and nod.) People who put a lot of thought into cultivating otherness find it hard to resist when someone says, "You have a remarkable sense of style; tell me about your clothes, haircut, ink, piercings, turban, monocle, clown shoes, or iguana."

When outsider appearances aren't invitations, they may be warnings. Sometimes kids want to appear dangerous so people will leave them alone, and they won't be disappointed or otherwise hurt as they've been in the past. That strategy is a means of self-selecting *out* in order to preempt being rejected and *put out*. The outward appearance says, in effect, "Let me just make it easy for you to distance yourself from me on superficial grounds so I can distance myself from the disappointment of being rejected for who I am as a person." *Where* outsiders developed the expectation they'll be rejected one way or another is a rich vein you can mine as you get to know them and demonstrate God's relentless love for them. And, just so we've said it, you'll *need* God's relentless love for them because they're likely to test you before they really, truly trust you.

Rejects

This category generally includes introverts and outsiders along with others who are excluded by their peers. The exclusion is usually based on superficial appearances, physical or mental disability, or emotional or social deficits. There are adolescent cultures in which it's a social crime to be fat or unusually skinny; where it's a public offense to be intellectually capable but relationally inept; where it's a relational deal breaker to suffer from attention deficit hyperactivity disorder, to be poor, or foreign-born, or a late bloomer, or dark-skinned, or any number of conditions leading to harsh judgments against people for whom Jesus "made himself nothing by taking the very nature of a servant, being made in human likeness." (Philippians 2:7)

If you ask me, it's just not okay for people who claim their citizenship is in heaven to treat others with disrespect. No one has to like everyone—or *anyone* for that matter—but when we're together, there are no rejects. That means no teasing about gender or body type or race; no teasing about age, ethnicity, hair texture, or intelligence; no teasing about wealth, poverty, sexual identity, or introversion; no teasing, period. Conspire with other youth workers and student leaders to make sure everyone in your group knows this: If the joke has a victim, it's not funny. Period.

JUST ALONE

Finally, there are kids who aren't so much loners as simply alone. They're alone because they're new in town or new to the group or because they're the only one from their school. Some are alone because all their friends are younger, so when they entered your group, they left all their friends back in the group they exited. Others are alone because they are "widows" whose older friends all graduated and left them behind (these are people who had amazing junior years and feel completely lost as seniors).

Lonely kids may need help to forge new connections in your group. That's almost a no-brainer; it just needs someone like you to create reasons for kids to hang out where they can talk a bit, tell some stories, and get to know each other. If there's cheap food near your meeting place, get a partner and start a weekly supper club 45 minutes before your group meeting. There's nothing like food to bring people together…

Consider engaging your "widows" by getting them to talk about what their older friends contributed to their lives. Then explore ways they might give the same gifts to younger kids.

22

ADOLESCENT CRUSHES

People get crushes.

I don't know why; we just do. Young, old, and in between, single, married, engaged, attached...we get crushes. And they don't mean a thing unless we behave inappropriately.

In which case, if you're a youth worker, it's entirely and painfully possible to find yourself in a compromising position with an adolescent or coworker. No, that's too soft. It's entirely and painfully possible to *put* yourself in a compromising position with an adolescent or coworker. It won't sneak up on you; you'll see it coming if you're even remotely aware of yourself. If it happens, it will be because on some level you want it to happen or because you deny you're tempted and fail to get out of harm's way. In either event it won't matter what you said your intentions were. It will be a mess of monumental proportions and turn the lives of everyone it touches upside down. It's so not worth it. Oh, and by the way, it's a criminal offense.

Don't spend time in private with an adolescent you're attracted to—even a little bit. She may be shaped like a woman, may sound and behave very much like a woman, but she's a girl. I'm told this sort of attraction is primarily a male issue. I don't know—I know it's an issue for *this* male. I also know there have been enough disturbing accounts of female schoolteachers abusing male students to make me believe everyone should exercise caution and common sense, regardless of age and gender.

If you sense a kid is attracted to you, all the above goes in spades. The last thing you want to do is give him a false impression, right? That doesn't mean you have to be all weird about it; just confine your interactions to public spaces. And don't mistake your automobile for a public place. Driving that kid home alone after youth group could be very risky for both of you.

Does all this scare you? It needn't.

People get crushes. Crushes are little infatuations, little admirations, little appreciations for something good in another person. There is nothing inherently wrong with a crush—as long as you don't act on it. I know plenty of youth workers who have had crushes on kids in their youth groups—and kids who've had crushes on their youth workers—who moved quickly beyond their infatuations to enjoy healthy relationships because no one did anything inappropriate. Nobody has to freak out. It's just a crush.

When you have a crush, if you leave it alone—keeping your distance—it will go away like any other crush. Meanwhile, don't be too hard on yourself for being attracted to the younger person. It doesn't have to be a big deal, and it won't be a big deal unless you allow it.

If the crush doesn't go away, that signals an unhealthy attachment, which should be taken very seriously.

23

UNHEALTHY
ATTACHMENTS

A harmless crush on an adolescent is no big deal if you don't act inappropriately. Those crushes seldom even rise to the level of real temptation. If a crush does present temptation *(this is very important)* it's your responsibility to back off: no flirting, no solo time, no communication outside normal youth group programs until the crush subsides.

What's inappropriate?

- Peer-like attachment with a younger person is inappropriate.

- Sneaking around to be with a younger person is inappropriate.

- If you would just as soon your spouse or the person you're dating or the parents of the legal minor(!) didn't know about something you're doing or contemplating, you can be sure it's inappropriate.

- Actively fantasizing about a younger person is inappropriate.

- No matter who initiates it, any sexualized touch with a younger person is inappropriate. (If you're aroused, it's inappropriate—disengage.)

These aren't the kinds of things the leaders had in mind when they said they were looking for men and women with a passion for kids.

Don't try to muscle your way through an unhealthy attachment on sheer willpower; it will make you crazy and can put you and the adolescent in danger. Instead—

- Take a little time off for personal development—join an adult Bible study; take a watercolor class; learn a new software application.

- Create space for self-assessment—read and write and think; take walks and pray.

- Take a careful look at your rationalizations for inappropriate behavior—what have you told yourself to make an unhealthy attachment seem okay (or even virtuous) to you? *She's uncommonly mature....I'm trapped in a miserable relationship....He brings out the best in me....I would never do anything to hurt her....God put this love in my heart.*

- Would a reasonable person buy what you've been thinking? Would you buy it if you saw it between an adult and your younger brother or sister or nephew or niece?

- Seek the advice of a professional therapist or counselor to help you contextualize this attraction against the backdrop of your life.

I think our idealized images of the male and female forms suggest many of us suffer from arrested development—which is to say, a lot of us are stuck in adolescence. This is understandable inasmuch as that's when our senses were (pardon the pun) aroused by the emergence of our own sexuality. That experience is so intense, it's no wonder a lot of us remain perpetually attracted to the physical forms we found attractive in eighth grade (or whenever).

That doesn't mean we're all attracted to the same idealized forms—clearly we're not. But if you find yourself fixated on younger people in ways that make you feel inappropriately young again, you've got some unfinished business. This doesn't necessarily mean you're not cut out for youth work; it may just mean you're not yet mature enough to work with kids (no matter how old you are).

So thank God for the wake-up call and go do the work. Perhaps you can be a volunteer in youth ministry later. If not, that's okay; there's plenty of work in the kingdom of God.

24

THINKING ABOUT THE
BIG PICTURE

Like everything else, youth ministry occurs in a context that's larger and more complex than any individual or youth group. Coming to understand the rhythm of adolescent life will help you succeed as a youth worker.

If you fail to take that rhythm into account, you'll find yourself asking kids to make uncomfortable choices, and most of the time you'll be disappointed—not because they made the wrong choice but because you didn't understand the big picture and asked them to make a false choice.

Think of it this way: You probably have a job of some sort that has prior claim on your time and energy. You can't do everything you'd like because you have to show up for work or prepare for work or get enough rest so you can do your work. *School* is the primary job for your adolescent friends. I'm not saying schools are ideal environments for the real work of adolescence; I'm just saying five days a week through most of the year kids are required to show up rested and ready. (Okay, that's a joke; they're seldom truly rested, sometimes because they stayed up late getting ready, the rest of the time because adolescents, as a class, don't sleep well.) Be that as it may, they're required by law to show up and fill seats.

In addition to school, there may be after-school jobs...or sports, theater, music...or family obligations such as looking after younger siblings. In short, you don't own them. In fact, you may be third, fourth, or fifth on a list of very important relationships and activities.

What sets you apart from just about every other adult is that you don't have to be there. You're a volunteer, and on some level kids know that—meaning they know your performance isn't evaluated by how often they and their friends show up to meetings and mission trips; they know you invest evenings and weekends so they can do things they wouldn't otherwise be able to do; they know you're there because you want to be, not because you're paid to be there.

Here's something you have in common with kids: most weeks you spend something like 165 hours more in your "real world" than in youth ministry world. This puts you in a frame of reference to understand how important it is that youth ministry be about preparing kids for the 165 hours a week when they're somewhere else.

Sometimes pastors and others who are paid for their work with people have trouble remembering this. It's entirely possible you may see more clearly than anyone that youth group is just one slice of the pie.

25

(YOUTH GROUP IS ONLY)
ONE SLICE
OF THE PIE

Sometimes adults give kids the impression youth group is the most important slice of the pie. I'm not saying that's a thought-out strategy. But it's a message delivered early and often. Here's a way to help adolescents understand youth group in the larger context.

Draw a circle and invite your group to create a pie chart by identifying (in rough hours or percentages) how much time they spend on various activities in a normal week. Your chart will probably include these kinds of activities:

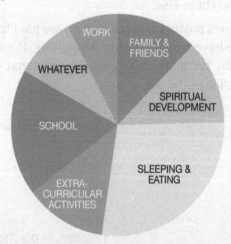

If you choose to assign percentages, divide the 168 hours in a week into the number of hours for each activity. For example, 42 hours of sleep divided by 168 hours in a week equals about 25 percent.

Once you've roughed in the activities and hours or percentages, here are some questions for your group:

- If we created a time-use pie chart for a group of students picked at random from your school, would it be significantly different from our chart? Because...

- Do you think a stranger with nothing to go on but this chart would conclude you are Christians? Talk about that.

- If the stranger asked about the hours you spend in youth group or other spiritual activities, what would you tell him?

- You don't have to answer this out loud: Would you be comfortable or uncomfortable if the stranger asked how your "whatever" hours reflect your faith?

For most of us the hours going to church or spending time with God don't result in a week-to-week schedule wildly different from friends who spend those hours on the Internet or sleeping in. So when we say God makes a difference in our lives, what do we mean?

What if we were to lay our pie chart over on its side—more like an actual pie with a crust and filling and less like a chart:

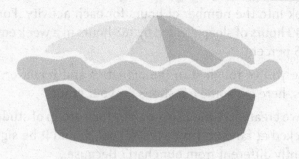

A couple of hours of youth group and some Bible reading might or might not make a difference in what kids talk about with their friends at lunch. But suppose the real difference between a youth group kid's pie and her neighbor's isn't the major ingredients—school, friends, family, sleep, and so on—but the fact that somehow the ingredients themselves are infused with God's presence? What if it turns out God is in the filling, in the crust—what if God is in the whole pie?

Christians text message and study and work after school like anybody else. We just do all those things believing God is somehow present in the details. I think that means youth group isn't an end in itself but a context for preparing kids to live the other hundred sixty-five, -six or -seven hours as if the whole pie matters to God.

That's what we're talking about when we say kids aren't the church of tomorrow; kids are the church of today. God shows up in the lives of adolescents when they're in places you and I can't go: classrooms, sports teams, artistic collaboratives. If the gospel is going to be lived out in those contexts, it's going to be peer-to-peer—exactly as it is where you spend the bulk of your time at work—exactly as it should be.

26

CLUTTER

(WE'RE NOT THE ONLY GAME IN TOWN)

Most kids are busy, and a lot of them are way too busy. Everybody wants a piece of kids' time, and some adults are in a position to demand it because they can give kids better or worse grades; because they can put them in the game or put them on the bench; because they can cast them in featured roles or put them in the chorus; because they can schedule them for good shifts, bad shifts, or no shifts at all. As a volunteer youth worker, know this going in or be prepared to learn it the hard way.

Learn the organizational rhythms of schools, sports, plays, part-time jobs, and the SAT. There's no reason to make a habit of competing with things that are legitimately important to kids and their families.

While you're at it, avoid counterprogramming against the rest of Christendom. The best time to plan a trip to the soup kitchen is probably not the morning after prom *or* the weekend of the church family retreat.

If you volunteer in a church, the events calendar shouldn't be hard to get your hands on. And hardly a school in America doesn't post a calendar online so students and parents can be on the same page. If you don't have access to the Internet, there's a nice person at the front desk of every school who has waited all day for someone to call or come by and say "please" and "thank you" about *anything*. She will be happy to give you a copy of the school calendar.

Next year's school calendar will be roughed out pretty well by the time school ends in the spring, including holidays, testing periods, and teacher in-service days. In-service days are good occasions to plan a day off to do something cool with kids (who often don't see in-service days coming until they're already there, so they seldom have big plans). You'll be a hero if you turn those unclaimed days into something memorable.

But here's a place to let yourself off the hook a little. Even when you keep an eye on the big picture, you'll never satisfy everybody's calendar demands. Sometimes you have to do what you have to do and hope the timing makes sense to as many people as possible.

And then there's summer (or whatever months your kids are out of school). Kids tend to stay up late while they're on vacation, so if you have the stamina, think about useful ways to fill some of those empty hours...say, nighttime bowling from 8:30 to 10 p.m. followed by coffee at Denny's or the Waffle House to discuss life, the universe, and everything.

27

FAMILY TIES (PART I)

Like it or not, families have dibs. So why not learn to like it?

Parents are not our natural enemies—any more than teachers, tutors, coaches, or dance instructors are naturally at odds with us. Unless something is very wrong, we're all stakeholders in kids' well-being. That doesn't rule out the possibility that some parents could find you a little threatening—especially if their kids make it clear they'd rather hang with you than spend time with the family. If you get that sense from any parents, look for ways to engage them by honestly affirming positive qualities you see in their children. Things are better all around if you don't come off as a know-it-all or competitor.

Of course we'd be less than honest if we didn't acknowledge that some youth workers have mixed feelings about parents. Who doesn't celebrate the importance of parenting as a concept? We all value high-functioning moms and dads and wish there were more of them. But anyone can see, some parents have poor connections with their children, some neglect their kids, some seem too strict, and some just don't seem to get it. So there are times in youth ministry when we find ourselves wanting to help, and other times we want to *be* helped—and sometimes we wish everyone would just leave us alone to do our work with students. Where these conflicts exist, you won't find them any easier if you happen to be young or if you have unresolved issues with your own parents.

On occasion you may meet parents who expect you to turn their children into high-functioning adults in a couple of hours a week. If you tell them it takes more than that, they'll ask how much more and happily allocate additional hours if that's what you need. Keep pointing them back to the big picture: Maturing is a complex process; in the long run (for better or worse), parents tend to have more influence on spiritual formation than youth workers. This is not a competition—we're all in this together.

A related complication swirls around the tension with parents whose values—as expressed in actual behavior, not just words—seem to be at odds with the values of God's kingdom. It's not uncommon to find adults who, like St. Augustine, want to become faithful and self-controlled, "only not yet";[10] whose appetite to give their children the good life sometimes overshadows the hope their children will live good lives.

The only solution I know for this tension involves seeing every parent as a work in progress, just like me, just like you. Most parents are not what they appear to be. They have their own pains and weaknesses just as certainly as their own strengths. They have things they've learned and things

[10] Saint Augustine, *Confessions*, 8.7.

they've forgotten and things they have yet to learn. Again...
that's just like the rest of us, so one thing no one can justify is
being arrogant toward parents.

Once in a long while you may encounter a parent who is
truly toxic, maybe even dangerous. Whatever you do, don't
jump to that conclusion easily—you should have hard evidence of neglect or abuse—but if you meet such a person,
take thoughtful steps to protect the child or children whose
well-being is at stake. You'll find ideas about how to do that in
chapters 15 and 16, "When What You Hear Sounds Like Trouble" and "Reporting Abuse."

28

FAMILY TIES
(PART II)

If you have a family of your own, they have dibs on you. Honestly, you gain nothing by letting your spouse or kids get the impression you'd rather hang with the youth group than spend time with the family. If they come to believe you're neglecting them in order to nurture other people's children... well, you have to admit that's the kind of thing that would be easy to take personally.

That said, I think there's much to be gained when your family sees you extend yourself to help adolescents grow up whole and healthy:

- You demonstrate what it looks like to serve the larger family of God—a value we all need our children to embrace and duplicate in their own lives.

- You demonstrate the value of serving people who aren't powerful in the church or society—something your children will come to appreciate as they grow older.

- You may be able to embody the notion of *calling*: I declined multiple nominations to serve in my church's governing body until they stopped asking—not because that's unimportant work but because I don't think it's *more* important than serving kids. By the same token, I wouldn't try to talk anyone into replacing his or her sense of calling in the church with mine. My wife married me for better or worse but not for girls' Bible study. This isn't because she has anything against girls' Bible study; it's because God put her to work elsewhere.

If the folks at home get any of this from watching you, it's a beautiful thing...as long as it's not at their expense. Which is a question of balance, isn't it? You'll face occasions when—borrowing a line from one of Andy Stanley's talks at the National Youth Workers Convention[11]—you have to decide whom you're going to disappoint. I'm not suggesting your family requires your undivided attention 24/7. I'm just saying it's a bad thing if they come to believe you'd generally rather be somewhere else.

Here are some ways to keep that from happening:

- Be intentional about reconciling your youth ministry calendar with your family calendar, not the other way around.

- Include family members where it makes sense—but guard them from feeling dragged along.

- Set sensible boundaries on how early and how late kids can interrupt you with visits, phone calls, and text mes-

---

[11] The National Youth Workers Convention (NYWC) has been a fixture on my calendar for more than two decades, sometimes because I have something to do there (a workshop or whatever), but always because I want to be there with people who take kids seriously and work to help them grow up healthy and whole. Learn about the next NYWC at www.YouthSpecialties.com.

sages. It's okay to temporarily suspend those boundaries under crisis conditions—sometimes I've found it useful to tell an adolescent or parent, "I've let Susan know I'm keeping my cell phone next to the bed for the duration of this crisis. You can call me any time you need help while you get this sorted out." That's a subtle reminder of how seriously I take crisis and how important I think it is to establish thoughtful rhythms in day-to-day life.

- Be intentional about planning nights (mornings, weekends, whatever) off from your youth ministry activities to do things that matter with your family. In the long run saying, "It's my daughter's first game, but I'm here tonight because I really care about you guys," is not nearly as useful—for your daughter or your group—as saying, "I won't be here next week because I'm going to my daughter's first game. But it's all good because X will be here to keep you guys from burning down the house."

When youth group kids see you treat your family well, they'll get an idea of what it means to love Jesus and serve people—beginning with your own household. And maybe you'll be the first one they know who lives that out...and maybe they'll follow in your footsteps.

WHO'S THE BOSS?
LEADING WHILE FOLLOWING

You're probably not absolutely-in-charge-no-questions-asked and that's the final word about that. You probably report to someone — a paid staff member, a superintendent, a coordinator, a committee — who reports to someone as well. If you report to someone who reports to someone, and you don't know who that is, it might be a good idea to find out.

When you know who's the boss, it's useful to figure out who the boss is. He or she or they almost certainly have at least one thing in common with you: they want to help kids. Like everybody else, people in charge have strengths and weaknesses and hopes and fears...the whole bundle. Find out what that bundle looks like in the life of your boss. For example, he may or may not have the cultural and relational tools to do what you do for adolescents (and it would be good to know one way or the other). Get him talking about the highs and lows and dreams and expectations of youth ministry. Find out what attracts him to youth ministry and how he got where he is right now. Ask what he what he thinks are the biggest needs in youth

29

WHO'S THE BOSS?
LEADING WHILE FOLLOWING

You're probably not absolutely-in-charge-no-questions-asked-and-that's-the-final-word-about-that. You probably report to someone—a paid staff member, a superintendent, a coordinator, a committee—who reports to someone as well. If you report to someone who reports to someone, and you don't know who that is, it might be a good idea to find out.

When you know who's the boss, it's useful to figure out who the boss *is*. He or she or they almost certainly have at least one thing in common with you: they want to help kids. Like everybody else, people in charge have strengths and weaknesses and hopes and fears...the whole bundle. Find out what that bundle looks like in the life of your boss. For example, he may or may not have the cultural and relational tools to do what you do for adolescents (and it would be good to know one way or the other). Get him talking about the highs and lows and dreams and expectations of youth ministry. Find out what attracts him to youth ministry and how he got where he is right now. Ask what he thinks are the biggest needs in youth ministry and what he's asking God to accomplish where you are. And be prepared, in turn, to answer the questions you're asking.

Here are seven things your boss(es) will appreciate.

DEPENDABILITY

Identify what you believe you can contribute in time, relationships, and concrete deliverables (such as music leadership or Web site design), then do your best to keep your word. If on occasion you can't deliver, be up front about that and give as much advance notice you can.

INITIATIVE

If you have a bright idea, coordinate what you want to do with the boss, then go for it. If you want to start a Bible study, or organize a hike, or call all the people who haven't been around for six weeks, or get kids involved making sandwiches for homeless people, do the necessary homework, inform the boss of your intentions, adjust where appropriate, and get on with it. That order is important simply because it makes sense to be sure what you want to do 1) doesn't compete with the mission of your group and 2) isn't a harebrained scheme that sounds good in your head but is impossible to deliver.

ACCOUNTABILITY

Expect to be accountable to the rules of the organization and the laws that govern activities involving adolescents. This includes agreeing to have your name checked against the sex offender registries (if your group doesn't do this, encourage them to start now). Don't put kids at risk by encouraging or permitting them to do illegal, humiliating, dangerous, or dumb things. And if you make a mistake, own it, apologize for it, make amends if you can, and move on.

Another Set of Eyes and Ears

You can be a weathervane to help the boss know which way the wind is blowing. This isn't about gossiping or breaking confidence with kids or other volunteers; it's about generously communicating what you see and hear in as realistic a way as you can. Don't leave the boss hanging for lack of information you can give. At the same time beware the temptation to use your knowledge as a source of power. Nobody wins that game.

Feedback

Let the boss know how she's doing. Keep her honest by telling the truth about how things look from where you stand. Offer direct but generous critique of systems, program elements, and communications that aren't as good as they might be. Affirm the boss for what she does well. If things are falling apart, give her a pat on the back, a shoulder to cry on, and a helping hand. Don't let a good thing pass without comment any more than a not-so-good thing. Treat the boss like a teammate who needs to know what you know. Don't behave like a know-it-all.

When there's a problem, be the one to put in on the table. If kids are mad, don't let them just complain; help them express their anger clearly so it can be addressed. If parents are dissatisfied, don't let them gossip; insist they say their piece directly to the boss (and help them do that where there's an imbalance of power). If you're discontent, don't sulk and don't undermine the program and don't slink away. Get it said out loud and plainly. If you can't find a way to make that happen, then put it in a letter. Never go over the boss' head until you've done your best to address a problem directly and been rebuffed at least twice.

MORE WHERE YOU CAME FROM

The boss will really appreciate it if you recruit other qualified people to the cause. And face it—you're as well qualified to bring in new youth workers as anyone because you know what it takes to do the job.

30

IF YOU'RE IN CHARGE

You may be the expert and chief practitioner in youth ministry at your church. If so, thanks from all of us who know if it weren't for you, very little would be going on explicitly for kids.

If you haven't already done this, take a little time to define what youth ministry can and should be in your context. You don't need anything but an open mind and a stack of blank 3 x 5 cards to do this. Recruit some thinking partners to help you brainstorm about what you could be doing. They don't have to be youth workers; they just need to be interested in kids and willing to be part of a creative team for an evening. Include an adolescent or two if only to keep you honest. That said, be aware of the importance of addressing both *felt needs*—what kids know they want—and *unfelt needs* —things you're convinced kids would want if they had the experience and wisdom to ask for them.

CREATIVE THINKING

Start with a stack of 3 x 5 cards and some black marking pens. Ask everyone to write as many ideas as they can think of—one idea per card—about what youth ministry could include where you live. Each card should answer the question: "What could youth ministry look like here and now?"

At this stage of the game any idea is acceptable, and the *quantity* of ideas you come up with today will affect the *quality* of your ultimate plan. So for now more ideas are better than well-formed ideas—you can separate *could* from *should* later on.

Here are some categories to light up your brainstorming:

- Needs
- People
- Places
- Times
- Resources
- Programs
- Activities
- Communication

When the ideas start slowing down, try "five-sensing" your youth ministry dreams. What are the *sounds, tastes, aromas, textures,* and *sights* you can imagine in your youth group?

Hold your objections. At this point in the creative process don't let anyone say, "We can't afford that" or, "That would never work here" or, "We tried that before." You can all say those things eventually, just not yet. One of the secrets behind brainstorming is: The quality of your ultimate plan is strongly related to the quantity of ideas you consider (and in large part end up discarding). Don't worry about a bad idea getting past the group. All the really bad ideas will be taken care of in the next step.

When you think you've exhausted your group's imagination about what youth ministry could look like where you live, take a break. Ten minutes will do, but you can knock off for a week if you need to.

The point now is to prepare yourselves to enter critical thinking mode. If you pin your 3 x 5 cards on a bulletin board or spread them on a table, the collection of ideas might look something like this.

NEEDS	PEOPLE	PLACES	TIMES	RESOURCES	PROGRAMS		COMMUNI-CATION
NEED	PERSON	PLACE	TIME	RESOURCE	ACITVITY	AUDIENCE	MESSAGE
NEED	PERSON	PLACE	TIME	RESOURCE	ACITVITY	AUDIENCE	MESSAGE
NEED	PERSON	PLACE	TIME	RESOURCE	ACITVITY	AUDIENCE	MESSAGE

	SIGHT	SOUND	TASTE	TEXTURE	AROMA
	SIGHT	SOUND	TASTE	TEXTURE	AROMA
5-SENSING	SIGHT	SOUND	TASTE	TEXTURE	AROMA
	SIGHT	SOUND	TASTE	TEXTURE	AROMA

CRITICAL THINKING

Look at all the cards you wrote together and start throwing away the ones that don't answer a new, slightly different question: "What do we *want* youth ministry to look like here and now?"

Plenty of ideas that might be good in another context are simply not right for you here and now. Some of those not-quite-good-enough ideas come from the past and are worn-out. Others come from different locations and subcultures and don't transfer easily. Still others require people with different skills and gifts than you have. Set them aside gently but decisively—at least for now. Some ideas that don't fit today may work later as things develop and other leaders come alongside you.

Negotiate differences of opinion by adding, subtracting, or combining ideas. Don't get stuck. If you see that happening, set aside the disputed idea and say something like, "Let's see if we get clarity on this question as we sort through other ideas. One way or another, we'll come back to this later."

When the process is done, you'll have an outline of what your creative team has imagined for youth ministry, and it shouldn't be too hard to turn the surviving cards into action items.

Pray over the whole thing. Thank the creative team for their contribution. Ask them to tell you if they want to help with refining and rolling out the plan. Then write it up and share it with others you believe can help you succeed—ask them if they see any holes (and, by all means, ask for their help directly and indirectly).

Out of all the things I might have written about being in charge, I wrote this because you can use this process to retrofit, rethink, improve, or correct what you're already doing—and because I think it can make the difference between wanting to do good youth ministry and *planning* to do good youth ministry. Go through this process every year to help you filter through what you *could* do and zero in on what you *should* do.

REINFORCEMENTS: CALLING FOR HELP WHEN YOU NEED IT

If you're happily tending to the development of a handful of adolescents, you can ignore this.

But if you're spread a little thin—or if you want to reach out to more students—sooner or later you'll wish you had a partner. If only so you can take a vacation without feeling like you're letting everyone down.

Sometimes the desire to call in reinforcements emerges when a youth worker learns to say "enough." You can't do everything. You don't have to do everything. God has not called you to do everything. Please don't try to do everything.

There are other reasons for finding a partner (or two or three):

- adding skills and gifts to the mix
- including someone of the other gender
- broadening the age range
- involving someone of another ethnicity or race

31

REINFORCEMENTS: CALLING FOR HELP WHEN YOU NEED IT

If you're happily tending to the development of a handful of adolescents, you can ignore this.

But if you're spread a little thin—or if you want to reach out to more students—sooner or later you'll wish you had a partner, if only so you can take a vacation without feeling like you're letting everyone down.

Sometimes the desire to call in reinforcements emerges when a youth worker learns to say "enough." You can't do everything. You don't have to do everything. God has not called you to do everything. Please don't try to do everything.

There are other reasons for finding a partner (or two or three):

- adding skills and gifts to the mix
- including someone of the other gender
- broadening the age range
- involving someone of another ethnicity or race

- in case you get hit by a bus
- because someone who's simply not *you* might reach kids you're not reaching
- because youth work is just too important (and too much fun) to keep to yourself

If you don't have a better idea, start your search for teammates by asking a few adolescents to name adults they think really like kids. You might be surprised by the answers you get.

- Get some face time with people you think may be qualified and interested.
- Describe what you've done so far.
- Tell them how you came up with their names.
- Ask about their interest in adolescents.
- Tell them what sort of help you need.
- Describe the organizational policies or practices you've agreed to.
- Invite questions.
- Ask if they have any problem with your checking for their names on the sex offender registry.
- If it seems right, ask them to pray about joining you.
- Promise to get back with them in a week.
- Check for their names in the sex offender registry.
- Get back with them in a timely manner.

HOW TO VOLUNTEER LIKE A PRO

When I was a card-carrying youth ministry professional, I expected to talk with 10 people in order to get three or four who landed and stuck. Your mileage may vary.

If you've been working solo, you can take this to the bank: When someone joins you as a partner, her presence will change things—almost certainly for the better. You can also count on finding out how serious you are about helping kids no matter who gets the credit. Lean into it. Take your time. Give the partnership a chance to blossom and begin bearing fruit (not because working together is easier—it may not be in the beginning—but because it's the sane thing to do if your objective is nurturing young disciples).

32

YOUTH GROUP KIDS OR DISCIPLES?

Young Life's '70s-era corporate biography was titled *It's a Sin to Bore a Kid,* based on a quote from Jim Rayburn, Young Life's founder: "It's a sin to bore a kid with the gospel." I like that but it stings a little, too. I haven't always succeeded at really engaging kids in youth ministry, and I've watched in frustration as they "wasted" their discretionary time in "less significant" pursuits. Why would they choose those things instead of my things?

An easy and attractive answer is their friends are there, or the activity is sponsored by a teacher who will also be grading them in a class. A harder answer is that those kids know they're necessary to the successful completion of whatever task their club or team or group takes on. And they know their presence is far from essential to the success of my youth ministry programs. (See what I did there? *My* youth ministry programs?) It doesn't take a rocket scientist to figure out people go where they feel needed.

Whatever made me think I didn't need kids to be anything but an audience?

Well, for one thing, it was easier. Truly *involving* students is more difficult and less predictable than doing it myself. But that's not the only reason I failed to involve kids, and it isn't the first reason either.

For a long time I just wasn't sure kids were capable.

Today I feel foolish writing that because I was very capable as an adolescent. There wasn't a lot of adult direction when I began trailing after Jesus in high school, so my friends and I looked after each other—with some kindly adults watching from a distance, offering advice when we asked (and asking useful questions when we didn't). I suppose one reason I gravitated toward youth work as a profession is all the direct experience I enjoyed early on, when I made lots of mistakes under relatively low-impact conditions and learned more than I can say. I didn't have any sense in those days that I was a member of the church of tomorrow, waiting for my turn to make a useful contribution.

Decades later a friend said he thought youth groups were often more like what the church ought to be than the whole church seemed willing to be. He loved youth ministry because kids were willing to worship, pray, learn, serve, spread the good news, and enter into each others' lives more fully than adults. It's hard for me to argue with that. From where I sit, all that's beyond the capacity of adolescents is exhibiting the wisdom and stability that come with age (except when it doesn't) and contributing substantial amounts of money out of their own pockets.

What that misses, of course, is the energy that emerges from generational connections—the receiving and passing on of faith stories when we're all in it together. That's one of the dangers of youth ministry in isolation. I don't think it matters how good it is; if youth ministry segregates adolescents from children and adults, it creates the wrong impression about living in community—it ends up just like high school, only more so.

And just like high school, I'm afraid a lot of what educators refer to as "teaching" and youth workers refer to as "youth ministry" is done *to* adolescents or *for* them rather than *with* them and *alongside* them—with the result that kids grow up bored and disengaged, rousing only to be entertained or, more commonly, out of a sense of obligation or loyalty.

I think adolescents are capable of transcending the role of "youth group kids." I think they're capable of following Jesus as *disciples*—followers who aren't waiting until they're older to live in the way of Jesus. When they live that life, they serve out of the gifts of God's Spirit in them; they contribute as significantly as any adult to the real work of the body of Christ; they become partners in serving the world—and their own blocks—in the name of Christ.

In the end, many young folks gravitate away from what we like to think of as their spiritual homes toward places where they know they're needed, where they know they make a difference. I'm convinced we can reverse this flow in a heartbeat if we treat kids the way *we* want to be treated.

WORKING WITH KIDS (INSTEAD OF ON THEM)

In communication theory, a lecture diagrams something like this:

SPEAKER

FEEDBACK (MAYBE)

The speaker says whatever she says, and each listener gets whatever s/he gets. All the messages go in one direction, and unless there's a chance for questions or some other kind of feedback, no one knows what's been communicated until the test is graded. From a theoretical point of view this is such a low-percentage transaction it's a miracle it works at all. But hang around most Christian organizations, past grade school, and you could get the impression it's the only thing that does work.

33

WORKING *WITH* KIDS (INSTEAD OF *ON* THEM)

In communication theory, a lecture diagrams something like this:

The speaker says whatever she says, and each listener gets whatever she gets. All the messages go in one direction, and unless there's a chance for questions or some other kind of feedback, no one knows what's been communicated until the test is graded. From a theoretical point of view this is such a low-percentage transaction it's a miracle it works at all. But hang around most Christian organizations past grade school, and you could get the impression it's the only thing that *does* work.

Lecture, to be plain, is the primary tool for working on kids.

The primary tool for work *with* kids is conversation where we employ narrative, reading, description, metaphors, images, a little bit of telling, and lots of questions and discussion. Working *with* kids graphs something like this:

The position of the leader in this kind of circle is not obvious. Each person can look each other person in the eye. Everyone can address everyone else. An outsider walking in on the middle of a healthy group discussion might assume the oldest person in the room is the leader, and he might be right, but he would have to watch for a few minutes to be sure. And that's not because the leader isn't *leading*. It's because leaders who work *with* kids ask more questions than they answer. They keep deflecting the attention away from themselves to others. They want kids to wrestle with the truth till it pins them.

In my experience the truth that eventually takes people to the mat is hands-on experience with the biblical text. Help kids learn to struggle with the Bible for themselves, and you'll help them grow for the rest of their lives.

My favorite method has always been to guide learners one paragraph at a time into an extended passage to see what they find there. The basic questions are simple, and if you're reading this guide from front to back, you've already seen them. They are variations on *what, why,* and *how:*

- *What jumps out at you from this passage?*
- *Why do you think that's significant?*
- *How does that change things for you?*

I try not to let what I know about a passage get in the way of what adolescents are discovering. I know I missed a lot when I first read the Bible; I'm pretty sure I still miss a lot when I read the Bible. Why would that be okay only for me? It's not. I'm not in a hurry to dump what I know on a group of adolescents. To do so may very well rob them of the chance to discover something for themselves if only I would keep my mouth shut for a few more seconds.

If we're not getting anywhere in a paragraph, instead of explaining it, I suggest we move on to the next one to see if it clarifies anything. I've learned not to be frustrated when kids barely skim the surface of a passage I love. The Bible is chock-full of time-release truth—and what doesn't dawn on my young friends now will be waiting for them when they come back later.

Which is the point. People seldom reach the same place at the same time. Good youth ministry engages kids at their points of *readiness*.

One of my friends told me how mad she was at me when she left our little youth group for a big-name evangelical college: "Everybody knew so many more Bible verses than I did," she said. "We would get into these late-night discussions, and everyone knew more than me."

I'm relieved to report I didn't take the bait...She continued, "After a few weeks they'd used all the verses they knew. That's when I realized instead of teaching us verses, you taught us to read the Bible and find things for ourselves." And she thanked me.

34

POINTS OF READINESS

This will definitely be on the test: *People learn what they're prepared to learn, not what they're supposed to learn.*

I've adapted something I learned in the mid-'70s from a guy named Chuck Miller. He called it "levels of rapport" in his seminar—by which I think he intended to identify a series of relational connections between phases of involvement in youth ministry. I suspect Mr. Miller adapted his thinking from the sales industry, but I suppose it could have been the other way around (or maybe another way altogether).

In any event, here's how I came to describe some "points of readiness"—signified by the red lines—at which we have opportunities to work *with* kids (but never *on* them).

POINTS OF READINESS

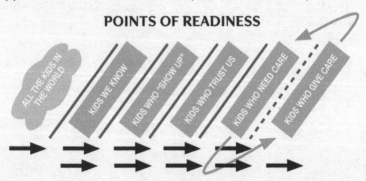

- "All the kids in the world" is a big universe. Over time you'll coax a few kids across the threshold between "all the kids in the world" and the set called "kids we know" just by virtue of being open for business. Each person's point of readiness will be self-defined: It might be a party, an invitation to study the Bible, a trip to a theme park, an introduction from a mutual friend...It could be anything. You can compile a "kids we know" list by naming all the adolescents you've seen in your group and all the kids you know from the larger community, including friends of friends. (I've never been comfortable counting people on a mailing list unless I've actually met them—you can decide on that for yourself.)

- From your "kids we know" list, compile a "kids who 'show up'" list. Ask, "When do these people show up?"

  - Youth group meetings?
  - Small groups?
  - Classes?
  - Barbecues?
  - Movie nights?
  - Service projects?
  - How frequently?
  - How recently?

- Ask, who are our mutual friends? (A lot of people show up the first time with kids you know who may be natural allies in reaching further into the newcomer's life. In any event, the thing that triggers a person's move from "kids we know" to "kids who show up" is her readiness to start showing up because she wants to—even when the person who first brought her isn't around.)

- The next list is "kids who trust us." You can pretty much move people to the "kids who trust us" list when they're ready to engage in a cluster of relational gestures...

  - when they ask you questions or offer their opinions outside of group discussions
  - when they see you in public and go out of their way to acknowledge you
  - when they call you for other people's phone numbers
  - when they invite you to sit with them
  - when they initiate a text or IM exchange with you

- Kids who simply show up may be using you to get something they want—road trips, a place to hang out, a chance to meet girls, whatever—so they sit through your silly discussions because that's the price of admission. The story begins to change when they start trusting you. That sets the stage for self-disclosure, vulnerability, and spiritual growth. When kids trust you, it's evidence you're beginning to have a positive influence on their lives (though, having said that, I know of kids whose trusted youth worker's influence wasn't all that positive, so...).

- From your list of kids who trust us, you can identify which ones are "kids who need care" and then which ones are "kids who give care." Of course, "kids who give care" are still "kids who need care"—no surprise about that; I still need care, and I imagine you do too—but "kids who give care" become partners in serving their peers and others who *need care.* (For what it's worth, I draw a distinction between kids who are able to give care to the very young, the very old, the very poor, and the very sick and those who are capable of giving care to their peers as an expression of spiritual nurturing that reaches beyond acts of compassion and charity. This may be a false distinction, but I think kids reach a point where they're ready to move on from lending a hand for their own benefit—to feel good or pad their college admissions essays—to helping others just because Jesus asks them to follow him on that path.)

When you identify kids' points of readiness, you'll have a better idea of where you are in the big picture; a better idea of how to relate to individuals and friendship groups; a better idea of what to expect from different kids and how to ask for it; and a better idea of what individual kids need and how to help them get it.

35

GENERATIONS

Every volunteer starts somewhere. Here's one man's path through life as a youth worker.

PEER LEADER

One definition of a *peer* is "someone who knows roughly what you know." That was certainly the case when I started leading my peers just months after beginning to trust Jesus. The connections I experienced in that context were immediate, sometimes uncomfortable, nearly always vital, and exciting. It was certainly hard to get away with anything. Putting on airs of super-spirituality was simply not tolerated in our circle. On the other hand, there was seldom any question of authority—I had none, needed none, was offered none, pursued none. What I possessed was what sociologists call *influence*—leading by persuasion and example. I lived in close proximity to the people I was learning to serve. They knew whether or not I was for real.

They also "knew me when." My friends could see my life changing in real time. I've never been more persuasive as an evangelist than in those first couple of years.

The biggest challenges to my effectiveness in peer ministry were immaturity and hormones. Immaturity allowed me to be very sure about some things the Bible isn't entirely clear about. That made me judgmental when I should've been merciful and emboldened me to speak sometimes when silence would've been more appropriate.

My hormonal situation was typical of many who are young and horny. I was trying to date people I was also trying to introduce to Jesus—a definite conflict of interests.

Still, my peer leader phase was a fruitful time in my life. I grew rapidly in relationship with God and God's people. And the kingdom of heaven expanded—at least a little—in the process.

OLDER SIBLING

About three years into my new faith, I made an unconscious transition to what might be called an older sibling youth worker. My youth ministry relationships were marked by the kind of interactions I've seen in reasonably healthy families. The older brother (or sister) influences younger siblings by treating them with humanity and offering his own life as a resource. My small measure of authority derived in part from the slight age difference and in part from my organizational affiliation. As an "older sibling," I was granted a degree of trust by parents and other adults. I was allowed to take kids on road trips and retreats. I learned the value of building relationships by doing things that required at least a nominal adult presence, for example, 16-hour days that began and ended at home and covered hundreds of miles in between.

I began "teaching" in the form of talking *at* kids. I wasn't very good at it, but I wanted to communicate what I'd learned about God so far. And there were some slightly younger kids who seemed willing to have me try. I suspect some put up with the lectures in exchange for something else they wanted (parties and road trips), some agreed to listen to me talk at Sunday School because it meant they didn't have to go to "big church," some endured it because of the long conversations we had at other times—and some were probably just being kind.

The big challenge to my effectiveness as an older sibling youth worker was inexperience. I didn't know what to do about conflict; I didn't know what to do for kids in pain. I felt helpless and alone when I talked with kids who were using drugs. I hesitated to go to older people for help because I didn't want to appear incompetent, and I didn't want to get kids in trouble.

I was beginning to get the idea that the adolescents I knew were in considerable pain, but I couldn't imagine most adults would know what in the world I was talking about. I felt something like an older brother caught between his younger sibling and parents.

On the hormonal side, I had to deal with little crushes going in both directions. It was during this period I began to learn if I did nothing about a crush, it would go away.

Good stuff happened in my older sibling phase. I was becoming somewhat more humble, and that made a little room for kids to see God at work.

Significant Adult

There came a time when I realized kids had begun treating me like a schoolteacher or an uncle—a significant adult. For those who liked me as a person, those were good connections. With others the transition meant finding new ways of relating—especially around conflict.

My self-identity was a bit tenuous in those years. I didn't want to lose my standing with kids *or* adults. I was afraid of being too directive, and yet I was beginning to formulate where and how I wanted to lead kids.

Perhaps my biggest challenge in this phase was, as a husband and parent myself, struggling to work smarter instead of harder. If I failed to think ahead, things I took for granted when I was a little younger—the marathon road trips and regular late nights—came at the expense of my wife and child. I seldom planned ahead.

I was also slow to involve other adults. My pride and my failure to see the big picture encouraged me to be a lone ranger for too long. We would all have been better off if I'd recruited more help sooner.

But I added skills and a certain amount of wisdom during this time, and I seemed to be the right person at the right time to help people grow. Today a few relationships that grew with kids during my significant adult phase endure in a way earlier relationships don't.

Somebody's Mom Or Dad

Eventually, I turned into *somebody's dad*. I don't know when it happened, but I remember the night I realized it.

I thought I recognized a tiny attraction from a girl who was brand-new to the youth group. It was Sunday night—her third or fourth time at church—and she was pretty flirty in the church sanctuary. I braced myself and was glad a lot of people were around until the flirting took a hard left turn: "Would you, uh, ever consider going out with my mother?"

What a great moment! Her friend almost yelled at her: "He's married!" What can I say? She was new; she didn't know. A page had turned...I was officially old.

The great thing about being somebody's dad was the growing confidence between kids and me. They began trusting me with their pain in ways I hadn't been prepared to deal with in my older sibling and significant adult periods. I started to understand that kids expected me to have a point of view. When they came to meetings, they didn't want to waste time—they wanted to know what I knew about God. I started to gain skill at engaging kids in dialogue by asking good questions. I came to appreciate the strength of diversity, and I enjoyed working with other adults. The differences that threatened me before now felt like complements among the youth ministry team.

Parent

Then one day I was a peer with the parents of adolescents. The kids saw it first, I think. They began treating me like a parent in the best sense of the word. They confided in me, asked for insight and advice, came to me when they were in pain.

Kids told me things they apparently weren't telling other people. I became an advocate for adolescents in adult conversations and an advocate for parents with their kids. Someone asked, "How do you get kids to tell you those things?" My answer was deceptively simple: "I listen."

I saw my own child approaching the group I led, and I thought long and hard about what that might mean for us. I was unwilling to sacrifice Kate's experience in high school to prolong my continuing high school ministry—I didn't tell Kate that; I just kept my eyes open.

I needn't have worried. Kate blended into the group as naturally as anyone else. I was able to separate my dad stuff from my youth worker stuff. Later, when Kate found out I'd considered taking some time off to make room for her, she was a little indignant.

The picture changed when I left my job as a professional youth worker and reentered the world of volunteerism. As Kate and I started over again in a new youth group, we both had to build relationships from scratch. The group was large enough for us to strike out in different directions, so we weren't jockeying for position or anything. But Kate had to deal with a unique consideration—*what if they don't like my dad and I have to kill them?* Fortunately, kids welcomed me, so Kate was able to continue high school and avoid being tried as an adult.

GRANDPARENT

As far as I know, I'm still in the parent phase as a youth worker—but I look forward to the transition I know will come one day: grandparent. I've observed a few grandparent youth workers, and it appears to be as rich as any other phase. If today I'm somewhat more objective than an adolescent's actual mom or dad, then as a grandparent I believe I'll have even greater clarity. If I've grown less prone to judgment, less easily shocked, less likely to panic as the years have passed, as a grandparent in youth ministry, I expect to have mellowed into a person who can apply deeper wisdom with greater consistency.

One of the things a grandparent can bring to youth ministry is a humble long-term self-assessment. She knows where she made mistakes and where she succeeded and how she grew and how she's growing. The grandparent has less to lose and more to gain by telling the truth than at any earlier phase of life. She also has greater access to the best youth ministry tool ever devised: the story. She knows what Douglas Coupland's character means in *Generation X* when she says it's not healthy to live life as a succession of isolated little cool moments: "Either our lives become stories, or there's just no way to get through them."[12] Our stories, generously told, give our young friends hope for the future. A grandparent knows this.

People talk about being too old for youth ministry. I don't believe it. One must simply change styles along the way. And how is that different from the rest of life? I can't do the things I once did, but so what? I can do other things.

I fear we have cut off the best years of youth ministry by defining youth workers as young, hip, energetic, and transient. Let's revise that profile and stay with the job for as long as God and kids will have us.

---

[12] Douglas Coupland, *Generation X* (New York: St. Martin's Griffin, 1991), 8.

SOONER OR LATER
EVERYONE LEAVES

For most of my adult life I've been just a few months away from mild grief, even if no one is dying. I find myself getting little, hed to a group of swell kids, knowing they have to go away soon. Of course, they also get to go away. My grief is mixed with joy for their success and gratitude for God's work among us. So I'm happy as well as sad. Sometimes I don't know what I'm feeling.

If I'm going to be completely forthcoming, I have to admit, with the departure of a couple of classes, I felt a little relief. They were hard on the ones ahead of them and behind them. They took way more than they gave, and I was not that sad to say, "So long." (though there were individuals I knew I would miss very much). Still, all in all, June has been mostly bittersweet for as long as I care to remember.

And then there are the replacements, kids who were in grade school last week show up for the middle school group and—there's no other way to say it—they're children! That

36

SOONER OR LATER EVERYONE LEAVES

For most of my adult life I've been just a few months away from mild grief, even if no one is dying. I find myself getting attached to a group of sweet kids, knowing they have to go away soon. Of course, they also *get* to go away. My grief is mixed with joy for their success and gratitude for God's work among us. So I'm happy as well as sad. Sometimes I don't know what I'm feeling.

If I'm going to be completely forthcoming, I have to admit, with the departure of a couple of classes, I felt a little relief. They were hard on the ones ahead of them and behind them. They took way more than they gave, and I was not that sad to say, "So long" (though there were individuals I knew I would miss very much). Still, all in all, June has been mostly bittersweet for as long as I care to remember.

And then there are the replacements: kids who were in grade school last week show up for the middle school group and—there's no other way to say it—they're *children!* That has to be taken into account. The newcomers don't know what to expect, and what they're prepared for is probably less than what you'd like to give them.

By the early '90s I was doing a lot of discussion-centered work with senior high kids. They learned to talk about fairly deep subjects at relatively sophisticated levels. As each summer approached, I made a speech that went something like this: "The new ninth graders will be here soon, and we're going to have to bring them along over the next few weeks. Do you remember junior high? It wasn't like this, was it... I'm asking you to be patient for a while. Some of the new guys will jump right in. Others will have trouble in the beginning. A lot of these guys are still concrete thinkers—they may not get the metaphors you use. Some of them will say things you think are dumb. They're not dumb people; they're just young. Don't laugh at them. Make it safe for them and help them get up to speed. Does that seem fair?"

When we worked at it together, it didn't take long to establish a level of communication that worked for seniors *and* new freshmen. And before I knew it, they were gone, too.

THEY'RE BACK!

If they don't leave, they can't come back on their own. And when they do choose to drop by—whether it's for a few minutes or the rest of their lives—it's a beautiful thing. I have a number of wonderful relationships with people I've known since they were 15 and I was in my 30s and 40s.

If I had one recommendation about what makes that possible, it would be this: when folks come back after high school, treat them as much like peers as they'll accept; and continue doing this until they truly are peers. This may take a conscious effort on your part. There's a shorthand among youth workers that identifies people as "kids," maybe even "one of *my* kids," for way too long. If you want people to live self-sustaining lives of faith, treat them as if their relationships with God are as firsthand as yours—which they are. If you want people to stop looking up to you so they can look you in the eye, treat them as if they're capable of doing everything you do—which they are. If you want people to feel the freedom to revisit things you said when they were teenagers—things they may not have understood, things that may have made sense to say under the circumstances but you wouldn't say to them as adults—then treat them as if they have become adults, which they have. You may want to involve them in your youth ministry team for the summer or long-term if they're back in the community. See if you can identify where they fit—older sibling? Significant adult? And invite them in. Or you just may enjoy being friends, and that's...fantastic!

Respect the likelihood that God has other service in mind for people who were in your group as kids. Don't keep reminding them of what they were. They aren't kids now; let them know you're glad about that.

You, Too

And then there's your own departure. For one reason or another, you'll almost certainly move on one day.

The best advice I can give is, *don't just disappear*. Say goodbye as well as you can. Tell people what they mean to you. Talk about what you've learned. Share your future plans and hopes.

If you're being "fired," then graciously express your regret over leaving. If you're going away mad, do it with class. Leave by the front door and don't slam it behind you. Don't turn your exit into a brawl and don't slink away to lick your wounds. If you're given a chance to say why you're leaving, be prepared to express yourself directly and with dignity. If you're not given that opportunity, then write a letter of resignation. Explain yourself in even tones and sensible terms. Then let God do what God will do.

37

AMATEURS AND PROFESSIONALS: A LAST WORD

There's a growing demand for people who focus on the formation of adolescent spirituality. That need is driven by the number of children and adolescents who lack significant adult relationships, by cutbacks in school and community programs, by losses in church influence, and by the complexity and variety of youth cultures. Under the best circumstances youth ministry is something of a cross-cultural venture for adults. So it makes sense, all things considered, to train and commission men and women for careers in youth ministry.

That said, there are more than 300,000 local churches in the United States—not to mention parachurch groups such as Campus Life, Student Venture, Young Life, and dozens of regional youth ministry organizations—and nowhere close to 300,000 professional youth workers. The reason is simple: on any given Sunday the majority of U.S. churches have fewer than 100 adults present. Without getting into the question of whether that's too small or too big or just right, let's just note that it's what *is*. Not a lot of congregations that muster 100 adults can pay for a professional youth worker.

Going forward, it stands to reason youth ministry will be done mainly by men and women who volunteer to make it part of their service in the name of Jesus. Most youth workers will be *amateurs*—people who *love* helping kids grow. God willing, you may be counted in that number.

Don't quit your day job so you can *really* work with kids. Resist the notion that real youth work is done by professionals. That's never been the case and it will never be the case—real youth work is done by people who show up in kids' lives: old, young, and middle-aged; male and female; cool and geeky; trained and untrained. Sure there's much to learn, and yes, we get better the more we practice, but the central requirements are presence and compassion: the willingness to enter and redeem the suffering of kids.

Don't let anyone convince you bigger is better. Bigger is only bigger. There's nothing wrong with big but there's also nothing wrong with small. Deeper is better; truer is better; better is better.

Do what you can as well as you can for as long as you can because you love kids. And trust God to do what only God can do with that. That's all anyone can ask.